CROSBIE'S DICTIONARY OF
Riddles

CROSBIE'S DICTIONARY OF
Riddles

by John S. Crosbie
Illustrated by Janet Sutherland

H·A·R·M·O·N·Y B·O·O·K·S

New York

Inquiries should be addressed to:
Harmony Books, a division of Crown Publishers, Inc.,
One Park Avenue, New York, New York 10016

Printed in the United States of America

Book and cover design by Janet Sutherland

Library of Congress Cataloging in Publication Data

Main entry under title:

Crosbie's dictionary of riddles.

1. Riddles.   I. Crosbie, John S., 1920–
II. Title: Dictionary of riddles.
PN6371.C7 1980   398.6'03   79-23356
ISBN: 0-517-54038X (cloth)
0-517-540398 (paper)

10 9 8 7 6 5 4 3 2 1
First Edition

To my family,
for being a good sounding board
and not sounding bored.

contents

introduction

In which the Reader learns what caused this Book and of some of the Problems encountered in seeking to render this Great Service to Mankind.

The most important books in my immigrant father's life were those by Horatio Alger and Joe Miller. Alger told him that wealth would come to the man who always wore spats. Miller told him that family spats could be funny. There was no shortage of the latter even when Father couldn't afford the former.

Mother's solution for easing family tension was frequently a watery one; she would serve us all hot soup. It was usually chicken—which would cause Father to observe, "There you go, Ruth, chickening out again!"

That was Joe Miller to the rescue; Father seeking escape through laughter. In retrospect, I realize that in those days laughter was all that he could afford. It was the time of the Great Depression—every adult I knew seemed to be greatly depressed. My father should not have been an exception. The New World streets that he had heard in Ireland were paved with gold made for pretty hard walking.

Yet he was a man of unshakable hope. In fact, it was the conflict between that hope and Mother's firm belief that the worst was yet to be that caused most of their quarrels. Inevitably, I was drawn into the whirlpool of feelings. I seemed to be swimming constantly through her chicken soup toward the banks of his indomitable optimism. I was always awash or a-wish. It was a rather wishy-washy childhood.

During that period riddles first came into my life. I remember Father, confronted at dinner with Mother's best effort to make meat scraps go a long way, looking up from the steaming bowl that she had placed before him and asking, "Did you stir this soup with your left hand or your right hand?"

My mother, tired and unsuspecting, replied, "My right hand, of course!"

"Aha!" cried Father, grinning happily, "I thought so! You really should have

1

used a spoon!" It was ever thus with him: riddle-riddled conversation. Fortunately for Mother, more often than not I was the target.

Stew really seemed to give him something to stew about. Perhaps that was because it was such a frequently presented reminder that the only person who seemed to be making money out of Horatio Alger's precepts was Horatio Alger. One night, Father looked up from the bowl before him, stared at me from under his secretly combed bushy eyebrows and demanded, "Son, what could you say of this lamb stew?"

Since his tone had told you that he already had an answer in mind, the best that you could do was to become the world's youngest straight man.

"I don't know, Dad. How *would* you describe the lamb stew?"

He glanced at Mother to make sure that he had her attention and then delivered his line: "Much ado about mutton!"

You really didn't understand, but you laughed because you felt that he needed laughter. Mother merely smiled because she believed that what he really needed was control. Years later, you are in a restaurant playing host and you try his riddle on your guests. You discover that they share your mother's viewpoint.

Despite such rebuffs, I am fascinated by riddles. One of the things that my father's addiction taught me was to recognize the kinds of riddles that there are. To me, they seem to fall into three general groupings.

There are those that turn out to have very logical answers, if you listen closely to the questions. Then there are those, the answers to which are pure nonsense. And, finally, there are the conundrums. This large group is also non-sense-based but is characterized by a play on words being involved in the answer.

Thus, Mother would have survived his stirring riddle if she had not fallen into the trap of taking Father's question too literally. And I might have been a less gullible foil had I foreseen where he was headed with his conundrum when he took it on the lamb.

Sometimes you may feel that you just can't win when faced with riddles! Yet it is quite possible to do so, if you stay calm and don't lose your head.

It is hoped that this book will help. Since it is an attempt to present a comprehensive report on the significant riddles currently extant in English or surviving in translation, you can use it two ways—to make you an expert riddler or to provide a quick defense against anyone who feels that he or she already is!

Our conscientious editor has pointed out that here and there this sister tome to the *Dictionary of Puns* shows traits that remind you of their common parent-age. He is right. Many of the plays on words in the puns book were first dis-covered in riddles. However, not to record some conundrums here simply because the puns involved have been catalogued elsewhere would seem to be a weak defense for incompleteness.

As you plunge into this dictionary, we ask only that you do so with some respect for the past. Buried among the current riddles are ones that are thou-sands of years old. If you are, or become, a riddle addict, history provides you with good company—a king of ancient Egypt, the Sphinx and Abraham Lincoln have contributed to these pages, as have a host of others.

We make no apology for failing to credit all of them. As we said at the start of the first edition of the *Dictionary of Puns,* "If you steal from one author, it's plagiarism; if you steal from many, it's research." (Even that was plagiarized from

Wilson Mizner!) We have researched boldly among many current sources—only to discover, as we reached back in time, how often those sources were themselves echoes of the past.

If other riddles there be, please let us have them. This first attempt to present riddles of our times in dictionary form doubtless will be followed by subsequent editions in which we would be happy to give your contributions a home.

We hope that the arrangement of the topics alphabetically will provide the student and the casual reader with a structure that is easy to follow.

We also hope that the two groups of readers most likely to be offended by some of the contents will forgive us.

Occasionally, understanding a conundrum depends on playing with the accent of an ethnic or regional minority, as in the riddle where "vortex" is meant to suggest "war tax." In reporting on the existence of such riddles, we have not intended any slurs.

Similarly, while we have been conscious of the desirability of according equality to both sexes, we have been hampered by the English language's failure to provide some more suitable pronoun than "it" to correct the traditional dominance accorded "he" over "she." For that reason, we have had to live with our language's tendency to be unfair to the fair. Mankind remains mankind.

After all, the significant syllable is "kind." Not in the Germanic sense, for that would be childish, but because it also speaks of kindliness. Man is kind. Humans do have fun. One dividend from investing time in doing this book has been to learn that for our species virtually every quarter has been changed in some way by our scents of humor.

As you read what follows, I hope that you will agree. It would also be flattering if you were to concur with the answer to the riddle which my father might have added: "What can you say to a man who has compiled a whole dictionary of riddles?"

Surely, his answer would have been, "Riddle man, you've had a busy day!"

—John S. Crosbie

let's play riddles!

How to use *Crosbie's Dictionary of Riddles* at parties or simply as a source of fun among friends:

Two or more people can play. Each person or team takes a turn at selecting a key word from the book. The choice having been announced, a riddle containing the word is then read aloud. The challenged person or team tries to guess the answer given in the book. Other answers, no matter how funny they are, don't count!

The person or team challenged must respond within three minutes or pass. (An egg timer is a handy device for settling disputes!) Members of a team may consult among themselves. If no correct answer is given before the three minutes are up, the asking person reads the answer. The book is then passed to the opposing person or team to make the next choice of key word and riddle.

Each time a correct answer is given, the winner or winning team scores ten points. The first person or team to get one hundred points wins the game.

How to Win More Often

1. If an opponent chooses a key word for which more than one riddle is shown in the book, do not use that key word again during the same game, since it is likely that your opponent or opponents have read all the entries for that key word and may remember the answers!

2. As a general rule, conundrums are more likely to stump your opponents than other types of riddles.

3. You will find that if you make a note of each key word used and if the associated riddle was correctly guessed, you will soon build up an awareness of which riddles are the hardest and you can use these in subsequent games.

Note: The book contains riddles that will appeal to all age levels. If your group is young, it might be well to preselect the riddles to be used.

Q. When are **acrobats** allowed
in hotel dining rooms?

A. When they want tumblers on
the tables.

A

Why is A like honeysuckle?
Because a B follows it.

Why should men stay away from the letter A?
Because it makes men mean.

Why is the letter A like twelve noon?
Because it's always in the middle of day.

aardvark
What did the aardvark say to the ant when they first met?
"Pleased to eat you!"

abdication
Why is growing bald like abdication?
The hair is giving up the crown.

accidents
What is better than presence of mind in an automobile accident?
Absence of body.

acorns
What did the little acorn say when it was told the facts of life?
"Geometry!"

What did the acorn say to the walnut?
"I guess the oak is on me!"

acrobats

Why is an acrobat a handy person to know?
Because he can always do a good turn.

When are acrobats allowed in hotel dining rooms?
When they want tumblers on the tables.

actors

What is the difference between being an actor and being an undertaker?
If you are an undertaker you don't have time to rehearse.

What did the drunken actor say in the apartment house lobby?
"2B or not 2B?"

Why is a good actor like a good architect?
Because they both draw good houses.

What kind of actor do you think of when you hear the word "applaud"?
One who leaves the stage too slowly.

Who was the best actor in the Bible?
Samson. He brought the house down.

Adam

At what time of day was Adam created?
Just a little before Eve.

What was the situation when Adam ate the apple and fell from grace?
It was a case of cores and defect.

What was the real reason that Adam got thrown out of the Garden of Eden?
He raised Cain.

How did Adam and Eve feel when they left the Garden?
A little put out.

What was the world's first palindrome; the three words Adam used when he introduced himself to Eve?
"Madam, I'm Adam."

affection

When do boats become very affectionate?
When they hug the shore.

age

We have heard a lot about the Age of Aquarius. What is the Age of Leo?
Seventeen on his last birthday.

Why is a dilapidated house like old age?
Because its gate is feeble and its locks are few.

At what age should a man marry?
At the parsonage.

airplanes
Why is an airplane that has plowed into the earth like a successful land speculator?
Because both have taken a flyer in real estate.

When should you refuse to get on an airplane?
When its listed time of arrival is followed by a question mark.

alcohol
Why did the consumption of alcohol decline in Germany near the end of the Second World War?
The people weren't sure whether they could afford another juggernaut.

alders
Why is the alder tree so popular?
Stop aspen questions like that!

alligators
Why is an alligator deceitful?
He takes you in with an open face.

alphabet
When can the alphabet be shortened?
When U and I are one.

What letters are not in the alphabet?
The ones that are in the mailbox.

angels
What did one angel say to the other?
"Halo there!"

Why is it fun to be an angel?
Because when you get to heaven you will have a high old time.

anger
What makes the ocean get angry?
It has been crossed so often.

Why is anger like a pot of beans?
Because both can be so unpleasant when they boil over.

animals

Why do animals make such poor dancers?
Because they all have two left feet.

What is the Golden Rule of the animal world?
Do unto otters as you would have them do unto you.

What animal eats the least?
A moth. It only eats holes.

What animal can jump as high as a tree?
Every animal. Trees can't jump.

What animal can you never trust?
A cheetah.

What two animals go everywhere you go?
Your calves.

What farm animal has cannibal tendencies?
The cow, because it always wants to eat its fodder.

What animal do you look like when you take a bath?
A little bear.

Ann Arbor

Where is Ann Arbor?
Anywhere you can anchor safely.

anode

What is "anode"?
A shocking piece of poetry created by a positive Pole.

answers

I never ask questions, but I get many answers. What am I?
A doorbell.

If a soft answer turneth away wrath, what does a hard answer do for you?
A. It helps create a dictionary of riddles.
B. It turneth wrath your way.

antelopes

What is an antelope?
A family scandal.

Why did the antelope?
Nobody gnu.

antidote
What is an antidote?
A condition related (usually by marriage) to the Oedipus complex.

antifreeze
How do you make antifreeze?
You steal her blanket.

antiques
What antiques are usually worthless?
Antique jokes.

Why is an antique bought cheaply like the profit from selling drinks?
They're both a bargain.

ants
What is smaller than an ant's mouth?
An ant's dinner.

What is a foreign ant?
Important.

What are the largest ants in the world?
Elephants.

apartments
What is there about an apartment that seldom falls, but never hurts the occupant when it does?
The rent.

apes
What tool does an ape use to fix a leaky tap?
A monkey wrench.

aplomb
Can you give a sentence showing how to use "aplomb" in the political sense?
The job that Governor Spleen gave his aunt was aplomb.

appendicitis
What is the cause of appendicitis?
Information in the appendix.

appetite
Where would you send a man to get an appetite?
To Hungary.

What are the only two things you have to do to satisfy all your normal appetites?
(A) Eat, drink, and (B) marry.

apples

If your brother gets a whole apple and you only have a bite, what should you do?
Scratch it.

Why was it an apple that Eve offered?
She had no cloves.

What is the difference between apples and alligators?
If you don't know, I'll certainly never ask you to bring home apples!

Round as an apple and thin as a knife. Answer this riddle and I'll buy you a wife!
A dime.

When did the apple turn over?
When it saw the jelly roll.

How can you divide seventeen apples equally between eleven boys if four of the apples are very small?
By making apple sauce.

Arabs

How do we know that the Arabs are not in need of sugar?
Because they have been raising cane for years.

Quote the war cry of the Arabs.
"Prepare to meet your Mecca!"

If the Arabs are getting fatter, why is their gasoline?
Your gas is as good as mine!

archipelago

What is an archipelago?
A long run in music.

arguments

Why is a dull argument like a lively one?
Because it is all sound.

Why do skunks get into arguments?
Because they like to raise a stink.

arithmetic

Why should you wear glasses when doing arithmetic?
It improves division.

Ark

If all the other animals went into the Ark in pairs, why didn't the worms?
Because they went in apples.

armies
What do we need armies for?
To keep our handies on.

If, as Napoleon said, an army marches on its stomach, what do soldiers do when a march is over?
Stand up.

arrows
Why is a girl in love like an arrow?
Because she can't go off without her beau and is kept in a quiver until she does.

Why is the arrow such an old-fashioned weapon?
Because it travels in an arc.

art
What happens to you if you buy too much 17th- and 18th-century art?
You end up baroque.

artists
What sort of European artist tries to put some money away for a rainy day?
A pavement artist.

Why do artists really never need to be short of money?
They can always draw checks.

Asia
Why is Asia like a grocery store before Thanksgiving or Christmas?
There is always a Turkey in it.

What was the first play by Shakespeare to be produced in Asia?
Asia Like It.

assumptions
Name a safe assumption you can make from watching television crime shows.
Death is just around the coroner.

astronomy
Why do so many people enjoy astronomy?
Because it is so heavenly.

atheists
What is the best advice to give an atheist?
If you're browned off at religion don't sit in the puce.

Why is an atheist like a priest who is always late for services?
They both keep running into the church.

athletes

If an athlete gets athlete's foot, what does an astronaut get?
Mistletoe.

Why is a good athlete like a good piano player?
They both do better in the long run.

Atlantic, the

Where is the Atlantic the deepest?
At the bottom.

Why is the Atlantic like an idea?
Because it's just a notion.

Atlas

In Greek legends, Atlas was so strong that he could carry the world on his shoulders—but who was even stronger?
His mother—when she carried Atlas.

What did Atlas's girl friend say when they reached Africa?
"Atlas, we are alone!"

atonal

What is atonal music?
Music for which somebody is going to have to atonal the sins involved.

attention

If a man can't get a girl's attention with flowers, what else can he do?
He might try using enamour.

What is the difference between "Attention!" and "At ease!"?
"Attention!" is a gripper and a tease is a stripper.

attorneys

In what way does an attorney resemble a rabbi?
The attorney studies the law and the profits.

auction

What is the difference between an auction and seasickness?
One is a sale of effects and the other is the effects of a sail.

If you come to an auction at a crossroads, what should you do?
It's best to junction.

Australia

Which was the smallest continent before Australia was discovered?
Australia.

Q. Who is **bigger**—Mrs. Bigger or her baby?

A. Her baby is a little Bigger.

B

Why is the letter B like a hot fire?
Because it makes oil boil.

When is a man like the letter B?
When he is in bed.

Why does a narrow road like the letter B?
It will make it broad.

babies

Why was the baby raised on monkey milk?
Because it was a baby monkey.

What is the difference between a sixteen-ounce baby and a boy driving nails?
One weighs a pound and the other pounds away.

Why is a sleeping baby like a hijacking?
Because it's a kid napping.

What did the boy say to his sister after their father had explained how babies arrive?
"That's his story—and he's stork with it!"

Why is a newborn baby like a gale of wind?
Because it begins with a squall.

Where do baby elephants come from?
Big storks.

Rock-a-bye baby in the treetop.
When the wind blows, the cradle will rock.
When the bough breaks, the cradle will fall
And down will come baby, cradle and all.
A bird in a nest.

bachelors

Why is a bachelor like a sharpshooter?
Because he never Mrs. anyone.

How do we know that bachelors are bad at grammar?
Because they decline to conjugate.

bacon

What day of the week is best for cooking bacon?
Friday.

badgers

Why is a Scout Master like a badger?
When it comes time to pass out awards, he is a badger!

badminton players

Why are badminton players like canary lovers?
They're for the birds.

bailiffs

When you get thrown in jail, why should you yell for the bailiff?
Because he'll post your bailiff you can afford it.

bakers

Why is a baker like a beggar?
Because he kneads the dough.

When should a baker stop making doughnuts?
When he gets tired of the hole business.

Why did the baker's son decide to follow in his father's footsteps?
Because it was bread in his bones.

baldness

Why is a bald head like heaven?
Because it is a bright and shining spot and there's no parting there.

What does a bald-headed man tend to hide that he used to show everyone when he was a boy?
His top.

ballet
Why do masculine people tend to resist wearing ballet costumes?
Because they are just too too.

ballet dancers
When are ballet dancers hard on their families?
When they execute their pas.

balloons
Why is a balloon in the air like a vagrant?
Because it has no visible means of support.

balls
In which ball can you carry your shopping?
A basket ball.

How many balls of string would it take to reach the moon?
Just one. But it would have to be a mighty big one!

bananas
What can you make by putting two banana peels together?
A pair of slippers.

bankers
Why can bankers always hear the latest news on money?
Because they have a cash ear.

bankrupts
Why are bankrupts more to be pitied than idiots?
Bankrupts are broken. Idiots are only cracked.

What is the difference between a bankrupt and a feather bed?
One is hard up and the other is soft down.

Baptists
If you want to be converted by the Baptists, what is the first requirement?
You have to go from bad to immerse.

barber
Why do so many comedians start out as barbers?
That's how they learn to be cutups.

How should you greet a German barber?
"Herr Dresser."

barrels
Where are two heads better than one?
In a barrel.

baseball

Why is a game of baseball like a pancake?
Because they both need batters.

When is a baseball player like a thief?
When he steals a base.

Why do baseball coaches seem immoral?
They are always expressing their base desires.

When does it cool off at a baseball game?
When all the fans start going.

bathrooms

Where in France do all the houses have two bathrooms?
Toulouse.

baths

If a man crosses the sea twice without a bath, what is he?
A dirty double-crosser.

batteries

How do batteries get sick?
They get acid indigestion.

batters

What is the difference between a hard-hitting batter and a flea?
One's a ball smiter and the other's a small biter.

beach boys

What is the difference between a beach boy and a playboy?
A beach boy charges by the day and a playboy charges by the dower.

beaches

Why won't you starve on the beach?
Because of the sand which is there.

beanstalks

On which side of Jack's house did the beanstalk grow?
On the outside.

beating

What is hard to beat?
A hard-boiled egg.

Beatles, the

What did the Beatles say when they saw the avalanche?
"Here come the Rolling Stones!"

beaus

What two beaus can every girl have near at hand?
Elbows.

beauty

Why is a woman's beauty like a dollar bill?
Because when once changed it soon goes.

beavers

How can you tell from watching beavers whether or not winter is coming?
They start to build their dams at a beaver pitch.

beds

Why do we all go to bed?
Because the bed will not come to us.

What is the last thing you take off when you go to bed?
You take your feet off the floor.

Which is the best side of the bed to sleep on?
The top side.

What has a bed, yet never sleeps,
And has a mouth, yet never eats,
And always keeps a-moving?
A river.

beef

When was beef the highest?
When the cow jumped over the moon.

beehives

Why is a boy who upsets a beehive like a good churchgoer?
Because he is an earnest believer.

beer

Why should you be careful when you are drinking Swedish beer?
Two pints make one cavort.

bees

What did the mother bee say to the baby bee?
"Don't be naughty, honey. Just beehive yourself while I comb your hair."

How do bees dispose of their honey?
They put it in combs and cell it.

What attracted the queen bee to the Scottish band?
The drone of the bagpipes.

beetles
What did one beetle say to another as they started off for the barn dance?
"After the boll weevil all go home."

beets
If you were invited out to dinner and on sitting down saw nothing but a beet, what would you say?
"That beet's all!"

Why are beets like the remains of Hitler's armies?
The best part is in the ground.

belts
Why does a circus master wear a belt with three rings on it?
To keep his pants up.

How did a belt break the law?
It held up some pants!

Bengal Lancer
What is a Bengal Lancer?
What you get when you ask a question in Bengal.

Benny, Jack
Why was Jack Benny like a gossipy dowager?
He was good at telling stories but badinage.

best
Why is it impossible that there should be a best horse on a racecourse?
Because there is always a bettor.

beverages
What beverage represents the beginning of time?
Tea.

What beverages should you serve the visiting baseball team?
Lots of highballs.

bicycles
Why can't a bicycle stand by itself?
Because it's two tired.

Why would you push your bicycle down the street?
If you were late for an appointment and didn't have time to get on.

bigness
The more you take away from it, the bigger it becomes. What is it?
A hole.

Who is bigger—Mrs. Bigger or her baby?
Her baby is a little Bigger.

billiards
Why is a billards hall a good place to go to get well?
Because there you will come across some remarkable cuers.

birds
What is a bird after he is four days old?
Five days old.

How is a bird on a fence like a nickel?
Because it has a head on one side and a tail on the other.

What did the mother bird say to her anxious offspring?
"If you've got to crow, you've got to crow!

Why are birds such big eaters?
Because they take a peck at a time.

What bird is present at every meal?
The swallow.

Why do little birds in their nests agree?
If they didn't, they'd have a falling out.

What bird is a thief?
A robin.

If there are five birds in a tree and a hunter kills two of them, how many are left in the tree?
None—the rest flew away.

Why do birds fly south for the winter?
Because it's too far to walk.

birthdays
What does every baby get on its first birthday?
Born.

When should you kick about a birthday present?
When you get a football.

bishops
When does a bishop sometimes keep doubtful company?
When he walks around with a crook.

Why is a bishop like a porpoise?
Because he's at home in the see.

black

What is black and white and red all over?
A newspaper.

What else is black and white and red all over?
A penguin with a sunburn. (Would you believe, an embarrassed zebra?)

What is black and white and has sixteen wheels?
A zebra on roller skates.

Black within and red without,
Four corners 'round about.
A chimney.

What is blacker than a crow?
Its feathers.

blankets

Why is a blanket like an aspirin?
Because it's a counterpane.

What did the Texas rancher say to the blanket maker?
"That's quite a spread you have there!"

Bligh, Captain

In *Mutiny on the Bounty*, why was Captain Bligh content to pull for the beach?
His barque was worse than his bight.

blindness

What is the difference between a blind man and a sailor in prison?
One cannot see to go and the other cannot go to sea.

bloomer girl

Why was a certain type of girl in the early 1900s called a "Bloomer Girl"?
Because she was the type that pants after a man and then complains, "I bloomer chances."

blows

When is a blow from a woman welcome?
When she strikes you agreeably.

bodies

What has four legs, a back, and two arms but no body?
A chair.

booby

What is a booby?
A little bug that hides in flowers and scares bees.

Where do boobies come from?
The booby hatch.

books

Where do most of the popular paperbacks come from?
The trite side of the racks.

Why is a book like a king?
Because they both have pages.

Why is this book like a tomato?
Because it may be read but it can't be beat.

bookkeepers

What did the bookkeeper say when he got the wrong answer?
"It's audit hasn't balanced this time!"

bookstores

Why is working in a bookstore like being Moses in the bullrushes?
Because you're surrounded by all those great reads!

Boston Tea Party, the

How did the Americans get to the Boston Tea Party?
They were driven by British taxis.

bottles

What did the city boy say when he saw a pile of old milk bottles in the farmer's field?
"Hey, look at the cow's nest!"

boughs

I know a tree with just twelve boughs,
Yet space for fifty-two nests allows.
In every nest are birdies seven,
Thanks be to God in heaven,
And every bird with his own name.
What is the answer to this game?
The year.

bowling

Why is bowling like being divorced?
Because you usually have to pay alley money.

When does it pay to work in a bowling alley?
When you need pin money.

bows

What two bows can nobody tie or untie?
A rainbow and an elbow.

boxers

Why is an ex-boxer like a beehive?
An ex-boxer is an ex-pounder; an ex-pounder is a commentator; a common tater is an Irish tater; an Irish tater is a speck'd tater; a spectator is a beholder, and a bee-holder is a beehive.

If a boxer wants to put on weight safely, what should he eat?
He should go on an assault-free diet.

Why is a battered boxer like an alcoholic at noontime?
They are both out to punch.

boxes

My box is round; the key to open it is within.
An egg.

boycotts

What is a boycott?
A place where a baby boy sleeps.

brandy

Spell brandy with three letters.
B, R, and Y.

bread

Why did the visiting country girl go for a walk in the city carrying a piece of bread and butter?
She was looking for the traffic jam.

breakfast

What is the easiest way to get breakfeast before you get up?
Have a roll in bed.

What two things can you never eat for breakfast?
Lunch and supper.

breaking

What does not break, no matter how far it falls?
A leaf.

bricks

If a load of bricks comes to $500, what will a load of firewood come to?
Ashes.

brides

Why aren't brides allowed to wear their trains any longer?
Because they are long enough.

Why is a bridal couple leaving the altar like an ebbing ocean?
Because the tied is going out.

bridges
What is the shortest bridge in the world?
The bridge of your nose.

What happened when the Frenchman jumped off a bridge in Paris?
He went in Seine.

broke
If you're broke, why might it be a good idea to go out in the rain with your purse open?
There might be some change in the weather.

Brooklyn
What do they have in Brooklyn that they haven't got in Manhattan?
The Brooklyn end of the Brooklyn Bridge.

brooms
What is a witch when she's traveling on her broom?
A flying sorcerer.

brothers
You are my brother, but I am not your brother. Who am I?
Your sister.

For how long did Cain hate his brother?
As long as he was Abel.

Two brothers we are.
Great burdens we bear
By which we are bitterly pressed.
In truth we may say
We are full all the day,
But empty when we go to rest.
A pair of shoes.

Name the little thing that went forth alone and returned in a line with its brothers.
A grain of corn.

brown
Brown I am and much admired.
Many horses have I tired.
I tire the horse and weary the man.
Tell me this riddle if you can.
A saddle.

Buckingham Palace
Why is Buckingham Palace the cheapest piece of property in England?
Because it was bought for a crown and kept up by a sovereign.

bugs
What do you get when you cross a bug with an American flag?
A patriotick.

buildings
Which has more to tell—a tall building or a short building?
A tall building has more stories.

bullets
What did Mrs. Bullet say to Mr. Bullet?
"Darling, I'm going to have a B.B.!"

bulls
What did the bull say after he'd been to a china shop?
"I've had a smashing time!"

What flower most resembles a bull's mouth?
A cowslip.

What do you call a sleeping bull?
A bulldozer.

burlesque
What could you call the afternoon performances if you wanted to attract dowagers to your burlesque house?
Strip teas.

burning
Why is it better to be burned than to have your head cut off?
Because a hot steak is better than a cold chop.

burying
Why is burying an elephant a problem?
It is a huge undertaking.

buses
Name a bus that once crossed the ocean.
Columbus.

What happens to the boy who misses his school bus?
He catches it when he gets home.

bushes
Behind the bush, behind the thorn,
I heard a stout man blow his horn.

He was booted and spurred, and stood with pride,
With golden feathers by his side.
His beard was flesh, and his mouth was horn.
Such a man was never born.
A rooster.

businesses

What's the difference between the businesses of a trucking company and a store that sells notepaper?
One's moving and the other's stationary.

What kind of man really gets immersed in his business?
A swimming instructor.

butchers

Our butcher is 6'3" tall and wears a size 12 shoe. What does he weigh?
Meat.

What is the difference between a butcher and Santa Claus when they are both at work?
One is slaying and the other is sleighing.

Then why did the butcher put bells on his scale?
Because he wanted to jingle all the weigh.

What is another name for a butcher's boy?
A chop assistant.

Why does the butcher's wife always keep the books?
Because the business is a joint affair.

How does a butcher differ from a fashionable female?
One kills to dress and the other dresses to kill.

butlers

What did the judge's butler say to the caller?
"I'm sorry. His Honor is at steak."

butter

Why did Amie throw the butter out the window?
Because she wanted to see the butterfly.

butterflies

What butterfly is like a Russian naval commander?
A Red Admiral.

buttons

What goes around a button?
A goat.

buying

If you could buy eight apples for twenty-six cents, how many could you buy for a cent and a quarter?

Eight.

Q. Why did Lady **Chatterley** finally have to get rid of her gardener?

A. He was a bit too rough around the hedges.

C

Why is C the most dangerous note in music?
So many singers get lost on the high C's.

cabbages

An onion and a cabbage are having a race. Who's winning?
The cabbage is ahead.

Why is a good cabbage the most generous vegetable?
Because it is all heart.

cakes

What kind of cake would most small boys not mind going without?
A cake of soap.

What is the proper name for a small French pastry filled with bird meat?
Eclair du loon.

What becomes of the chocolate cake when your only son eats it?
It vanishes into the empty heir.

calamities

If a waiter carrying a turkey on a platter lets it fall, what three great national calamities occur?
The downfall of Turkey, the breaking up of China, and the overthrow of Greece.

calculator
What did the calculator say to the cashier?
"You can count on me."

calendars
Why is a calendar sad?
Because its days are numbered.

camels
What knights ride camels?
The Arabian knights.

When a camel was born with no hump, what did his parents name him?
Humphrey.

What do you get when you cross a cow with a camel?
Lumpy milkshakes.

canard
Why is a sensational report called a canard?
Because you canardly believe it.

canaries
What did the canary say when its cage broke?
"Cheep! Cheep!"

What do you get when you cross a canary with a lion?
We don't know but when it sings you had better listen!

candles
Which burns longer—a white candle or a black candle?
Neither. Both burn shorter.

What did the big candle say to the little candle?
"You're pretty bright for a little fellow!"

What did the boy candle say to the girl candle?
"Let's go out tonight!"

Why is a candle like an atheist?
Because it's wicked.

What is the difference between a candle in a cave and a dance in a roadhouse?
One is a taper in a cavern and the other is a caper in a tavern.

cannibals
Why should you always stay calm when you meet a cannibal?
It's best not to get into a stew.

What would a cannibal be who ate his mother's sister?
An aunt eater.

Why did the baby cannibal get punished for teasing the missionary's baby?
She wasn't supposed to play with her food.

What soup do cannibals prefer?
A broth of a boy.

Why did the cannibal feel ill every time he ate a missionary?
Because you can't keep a good man down.

What happened to the cannibals when they ate a comedian?
They sat down for a feast of fun but some of the food joked them.

cans
Why is a tin can tied to a dog's tail like death?
Because it's bound to a cur.

What did the can say to the electric can opener?
"You have a shocking way of making me flip my lid."

canticle
What is a canticle?
A little song that canticle your fancy.

caps
What goes all over the fields and leaves a white cap on every stump?
The snow.

If the captain left his cap on the capstan, where did the mate leave his plate?
In a glass of water by his bed.

captains
Why are sea captains always on their toes?
Because their training makes them good skippers.

cards
Why couldn't anyone play cards on the Ark?
Because Noah was always standing on the deck.

carpenters
Why did the carpenter refuse to hit the nail with his hammer?
Because it was his thumbnail.

Why do carpenters believe there is no such thing as stone?
Because they never saw it.

Why is a carpenter like a pilot?
Because they both know a lot about planes.

Why is a retired carpenter like a lecturer?
Because he is an ex-planer.

If you're hiring a carpenter, why should you choose one that is slow and careful?
He who laths last, laths best.

carriages
Who invented the first baby carriage?
The kangaroo.

What was President Lincoln's carriage called?
The landau "Hope and Glory."

cars
Why is an old car like a baby?
Because it always has a rattle.

How does a car go that has a horn, three wheels, and no brakes?
BEEP! BEEP!

Why did the rich man's new car remain undriven?
He advertised for a driver but had nothing to chauffeur it.

When is a car not a car?
When it is turning into a driveway.

Why should a freight car need no locomotive?
The freight makes the cargo.

cash registers
Why is a cash register like somone who can't pay his bills?
Because it is pressed for money.

cassowary
How did the cassowary bird get its name?
If you see one coming you should cassowary eye.

castaways
What is the one thing that you can be sure of as a castaway?
That you'll get a seat on the isle.

castles
Why does England have so many Tudor castles?
Henry VII always liked to have an extra exit.

catching
What do we often catch but never see?
A passing remark.

In Africa, they know of something you can never catch. What is it?
A breeze.

caterpillars
When does a caterpillar improve in behavior?
When it turns over a new leaf.

cats
What has the head of a cat, the tail of a cat, and is not a cat?
A kitten.

How can you tell one sort of cat from another?
By referring to a catalogue.

What is the best way for a cat to catch a mouse?
Eat cheese and then wait by a mousehole with baited breath.

Why is a cat like the sun?
They both go out at night.

What do you call a cat that falls in a pickle barrel?
A sour puss.

Why does a cat, when it enters a room, look first to one side and then to the other?
Because it can't look at both sides at the same time.

What makes more noise than a cat stuck in a tree?
Two cats stuck in a tree.

Why are alley cats like unskillful surgeons?
Because they mew till late and destroy patience.

What is the difference between a cat and a comma?
A cat has its claws at the end of its paws and a comma its pause at the end of a clause.

What is the difference between a cat and a match?
The cat lights on its feet and the match on its head.

caught
He went to the wood and caught it;
He sat him down and sought it;
Because he could not find it,

Home with him he brought it.
A thorn in his foot.

ceilings

What kind of room has no ceiling?
A mushroom.

What did the ceiling say to the walls?
"Just because you're a little cracked is no reason to get plastered!"

censorship

Why should they have censored *Gone With the Wind*?
It was a blew movie.

Why is movie censorship a dangerous thing?
You have no way of knowing whether the result will make censor not.

centaurs

Why were centaurs half horse?
Because they lived in damp caves.

center

What is found in the center of America and Australia?
The letter R.

centimeter

What is a centimeter?
A police breath-analyzer.

centipedes

What is worse than a centipede with sore feet?
A giraffe with a sore throat.

What is worse than a centipede with corns?
A hippopotamus with chapped lips.

What do you get when you cross a centipede with a parrot?
A walkie-talkie.

chairs

When the dowager asked her new maid to give her guests some chairs, what did the maid say?
"Hip, hip, hooray!"

Why is an old chair as good as new when it has been lost and then found?
Because it has been recovered.

When does a chair dislike you?
When it can't bear you.

champagne
Why did champagne become identified with seduction?
It is the wine of least resistance.

Champlain
Who was Champlain?
A Canadian who failed to keep the wolf from the back door while his horses were Champlain at the bit.

chanting
Why do the Hare Krishna people chant, ring little bells, and beat drums as they walk the streets?
It keeps away tigers.

charge
What was the charge when a sailor hit a man over the head with an oar?
A salt and battery.

How do you keep a bull moose from charging?
Take away his credit card.

What was the charge when the hermit was arrested for speeding?
Recluse driving.

Charles the First
King Charles the First walked and talked
Half an hour after his head was cut off.
How can you make sense of that?
Put a period after the word talked and a comma after the word after.

Chatterley, Lady
Why did Lady Chatterley finally have to get rid of her gardener?
He was a bit too rough around the hedges.

cheerleaders
How did it happen that the two cheerleaders ended up at the altar?
They met by chants.

cheese
If cheese comes on top of a hamburger, what comes after cheese?
A mouse.

chemicals
Which is the cleanest chemical in the lab?
Washing soda.

chicken
Why did the chicken cross the road?
Because Colonel Sanders was chasing her.

children

There once was a mother who had five children, half of whom were boys. What were the other half?
Boys!

When do children first begin to learn the alphabet?
When they discover what is not T.

What was it that Adam never saw, never had, and still gave two of to his children?
Parents.

I have a little child. When I run I do not catch it. But when I sit down it catches up with me.
My shadow.

chimneys

What will go up a chimney down but not down a chimney up?
An umbrella.

How many chimneys does Father Christmas have to get down?
He has to get down stacks.

chimpanzees

When does a chimpanzee chase a banana?
When the banana splits.

What is the difference between a chimp and a Chippendale?
A Chippendale is a styled shape and a chimp is a wild ape.

choirs

What causes the most scandal in church choirs?
When a soprano gives in to her bass desires.

chorus girls

Why are chorus girls like barge horses?
They have to learn to tow the line.

Christians

Why weren't the Crusaders typical Christians?
They were cross people.

Christmas

What will happen to you at Christmas?
Yule be happy.

What did the fireman's wife find on Christmas day?
A ladder in her stocking.

churches
> Why is it always so quiet in church?
> *People never talk above a vesper.*

> If you sing badly what should you do in church?
> *Refrain and let psalmody else.*

> On which side of the church does a tree grow best?
> *On the outside.*

> What tree is always found inside a church?
> *The vestry.*

churns
> Why was it that after Mrs. Jones had given her neighbor a butter churn, her neighbor gave her one back?
> *One good churn deserves another.*

cider
> Why are some people like cider?
> *Because they remain sweet until it is time to work.*

Cinderella
> What did the prince do every time he found a girl that he thought might be Cinderella?
> *He went down to defeat.*

circles
> Why is a circle of gold like the sound of a bell?
> *It is a ring.*

cities
> What is the nearest city north of Windsor in Ontario, Canada?
> *Detroit, Michigan.*

> Which Chinese city is like a man looking through a keyhole?
> *Peking.*

> What American city would probably sound friendliest to a Frenchman?
> *Miami.*

> What major city is almost wholly on an island that was once owned by the Indians?
> *Montreal, Canada.*

> What American city's name reminds you of a greeting in a nudist camp?
> *Buffalo.*

cleaning
How can you clean your clothes if you are on a desert island?
Throw them in the ocean. They'll be washed ashore.

Cleopatra
How did Antony first meet Cleopatra on the Nile?
He just barged in.

Why was Cleopatra so hard to get along with?
She was the queen of denial.

clergymen
Why is a clergyman's car like a king?
Because it is steered by a minister.

clerks
What is the proper designation for a stock clerk in a cannery?
Soupernumerary.

What did the Turk clerk say when he realized he and his friends had had too much to drink for lunch?
"Who'll tell the Bosporus?"

clocks
Why does a clock respond to its spring the way some kids react to school?
When it's taut it runs.

What did the digital clock say to its mother?
"Look, Ma ... no hands!"

When is a clock on the stairs dangerous?
When it runs down and strikes one.

How can you wake up in the morning without an alarm clock?
By listening to the bed ding.

What is the difference between a clock and a bankruptcy?
A clock goes right on after you wind it up.

clothes
What kind of clothes do Supreme Court judges wear?
Lawsuits.

clothing
What kind of clothing lasts the longest?
Underwear. It is never worn out.

clouds
What is the difference between a cloud and a kid being spanked?
One pours with rain and the other roars with pain.

coats
What coat has no buttons and is put on wet?
A coat of paint.

He has a red coat. There's a stick in his hand and a stone in his throat and he hangs around a lot.
A cherry.

Cockneys
Why do Cockneys drop their *H's?*
Because they're late H heavers.

cocktails
Why was the Wuthering Heights cocktail invented?
For people who always want just one moor.

coffee
When is coffee like the surface of the earth?
When it is ground.

coffins
What is another name for a coffin?
A snuffbox.

collections
When is a poor church collection like a policeman's helmet?
When it has just one copper in it.

colleges
Why is the first year of college really the best?
After your freshman year you sophomore.

colors
What colors were the winds and the waves in the last storm?
The winds blue and the waves rose.

What color is noisy?
Yellow!

Columbus
Why was Columbus a very dissipated man, according to Mark Twain?
He has been on a bust for hundreds of years.

coming
What is always coming but never arrives?
Tomorrow.

communism
Why does communism have so many people cowed?
Because they do it the herd way.

How should the progress of communism be measured?
By the nyet effect.

company
If two is company and three is a crowd, what are four and five?
Nine.

composers
Why is a composer of classical music like a sex maniac?
He is always making overtures.

conductors
What is the difference between an orchestral conductor and an oven?
One makes the beat and the other bakes the meat.

What is the difference between a railway conductor and a schoolteacher?
One minds the train and the other trains the mind.

Congress
Which member of Congress wears the largest hat?
The one who has the largest head.

conquests
The Russians used to ask, "What one thing can no man—not even the czar—conquer?"
Sleep.

constellations
What constellation is like a naked person?
The Great Bear.

contests
When the undertakers' association ran a contest, why was it a failure?
It was a dead giveaway.

contortionists
Why are contortionists thrifty people?
Because they can make both ends meet.

contracting
What things grow larger the more you contract them?
Debts.

conundrums
What is it that everyone thinks of when posing a conundrum and everyone thinks of when hearing one?
The answer.

When is a conundrum least like a girl?
When it is not amiss.

What is the difference between a person confronted with conundrums and a person facing a firing squad?
None—they are both about to get riddled!

cookies
A cook cooked two dozen cookies. All but eleven were eaten. How many were left?
Eleven.

cooks
Why should you be suspicious of cooks from Yorkshire?
They are always pudding you on.

When are cooks mean?
When they beat the eggs and whip the cream.

cords
What cord is full of knots which no one can untie?
A cord of wood.

corn
There were sixteen ears of corn in a barrel. A rabbit came each night and carried away three ears. How long did it take him to empty the barrel?
Sixteen nights. (One ear of corn and two of his own per night!)

Where do little ears of corn come from?
The stalk brings them.

What did Baby Corn say to Mother Corn?
"Where is Pop Corn?"

corners
What's found twice in any corner but only once in every room?
The letter R.

coroner
How do you become a coroner?
You have to take a stiff examination.

corpses
What's the difference between Chopin and a corpse?
One composes and the other decomposes.

costume parties
What happened when the young man went to the costume party as a dog?
He found himself curtailed.

counting
What's better than a horse that can count?
A spelling bee.

countries

Which country ought to be the richest in the world?
The Republic of Ireland—its capital is always Dublin.

What do they call a country where all the cars are pink?
A pink carnation.

When do you become a country of South America?
When you are Chile.

In what country do they let prisoners go?
The Congo.

courts

If you have to choose between going to court or going to a funeral, why should you choose the funeral?
Never put the court before the hearse.

cowboys

Why did the cowboy die with his boots on?
Because he didn't want to stub his toe when he kicked the bucket.

cowhide

What is the most important use for cowhide?
To hold the cow together.

cows

What route did the cow follow jumping over the moon?
She went the Milky Way.

Why do cows wear bells?
Because their horns won't work.

What did the discontented cow mutter to the milkmaid?
"Go ahead and try. See if I give a dram!"

Can you recall what happened to the cow that swallowed a bottle of ink?
She mooed indigo.

When is a cow not a cow?
When it is turned into a pasture.

Why did the farmer's daughter watch the lazy cows?
She liked to see the meat loaf.

What do you get when you cross a cow with a duck?
Milk and quackers.

coyotes
What is the difference between a coyote and a flea?
One howls on the prairie and the other prowls on the hairy.

crackers
What kind of cracker shouldn't be eaten with cheese?
A firecracker.

cradles
What did the cradle say to the baby?
"Let's have a swinging time!"

crazy
Why are vampires crazy?
Because they are often bats.

critics
What was the drama critic's comment about a stripper?
Some things are better left unshed.

crops
If a farmer can raise a crop of 250 bushels of corn in dry weather, what can he raise in wet weather?
An umbrella.

As I was checking Grandpa's crop
I saw something that made me stop.
It looked sweet and tasted sour.
Guess this riddle in half an hour!
Cranberries.

crosses
How do you make a Maltese cross?
Pull its tail.

crossword puzzles
Why is a crossword puzzle like a fight?
Because one word leads to another.

crowbars
What is a crowbar for?
To satisfy raven alcoholics.

Why would a man ask a woman to help him with a crowbar?
Because he can't lever alone.

crows
Why are crows the wisest of birds?
They never complain without cause.

culture
How do you know when you are cultured?
When you feel a tome reading.

Cupid
Why is Cupid a poor marksman?
Because he is always making Mrs.

cups
Name two cups from which you can't drink.
Buttercups and hiccups.

curling
Why did the man who was curling get stoned?
He played it too close to the best.

customers
Who earns a living by driving customers away?
A taxi driver.

cutting
Everyone can see you cut it but no one can see the place that is cut.
Water.

*Q. What goes **down** but can never come up?*

A. A well.

D

Why is the letter *D* like a sailor?
It follows the C.

When can the letter *D* be upsetting?
When it makes ma mad.

Why is the letter *D* like a wedding ring?
Because we cannot be wed without it.

daffodil

How would you define the daffodil?
A goofy pickle.

dairymaid

Why did the dairymaid quit?
She couldn't stand milking.

dairyman

What changed the dairyman's luck?
He found a whey to make money and now he's doing much butter.

daisies

What do you get if you cross a sheep dog with a daisy?
Collie flowers.

dance

What is the difference between a Hawaiian dance and a boa on the loose?
A hula is a shake in the grass.

What kind of dance do prisoners do when exercising in the jail yard?
The quadrille.

dancers

What is the difference between a dancer and a duck?
One goes quick on her beautiful legs and the other goes quack on her beautiful eggs.

dancing

Why is dancing like new milk?
Because it strengthens the calves.

If you are caught doing this dance, you will get the dickens.
The Oliver Twist.

dandelions

What did one dandelion say to the other dandelion?
"Take me to your weeder."

darkness

What is dark but made by light?
A shadow.

Davis, Jefferson

In the 1828 yearbook for the U.S. Military Academy, what prediction appears beside the picture of graduating Jefferson Davis?
"Most likely to secede."

days

Why is no day ever complete?
Because every one begins by breaking.

What day of the year is a command to go forward?
March 4th.

Which is the strongest day of the week?
Sunday, because all the rest are weekdays.

Why are the days long in summer and short in winter?
Heat expands things and cold contracts them.

What things, though they appear once in every day, and twice in every week, are only seen twice in a year?
Vowels.

Why was the first day of Adam's life the longest?
Because it had no eve.

deadlines
What is a deadline?
A funeral procession.

deafness
What is deaf, dumb, and blind and always tells the truth?
A mirror.

What letter in the alphabet is most useful to a deaf old lady?
The letter A, because it makes her hear.

death
If you were condemned to die, which is the best manner of death you could choose?
Old age.

The more it gets, the more it eats, but when it has eaten everything, it must die. What is it?
Fire.

debate
How would you define debate?
It's what lures de fish.

debt
Why is a man with a big load of debt like a man with a stuck car?
He doesn't know how to budge it.

When is a man over head and ears in debt?
When he wears a wig that is not paid for.

decay
How do you know that the wall is going to decay?
Because you can see its molding.

decimals
Why are decimals better than fractions?
Decimals have their points and fractions are often vulgar.

decree
What would you call the author of a church decree?
Canon fodder.

deer
What is the difference between a deer running from its chasers and a midget witch?
One is a hunted stag and the other is a stunted hag.

dejection
Why is a dejected man like one thrown from a cliff?
He is downcast.

Delaware
What did Delaware to the party?
Her New Jersey.

dentistry
Why is American dentistry a force for world peace?
Many people abroad are afraid of the Yanks.

dentists
Why are dentists artistic?
Because they are good at drawing teeth.

How do we know that a dentist is unhappy at his work?
Because he always looks down in the mouth.

Why is going to the dentist like enlisting in the army?
It can be a drilling experience.

Why did the man telephone the new dentist?
Because he was simply aching to meet him.

How does a dentist examine a crocodile's teeth?
Very carefully!

depth
Riddle me, riddle me, riddle me,
Perhaps you can tell what this riddle may be:
    As deep as a house,
    As round as a cup,
And all the king's horses can't draw it up.
A well.

dessert
What dessert represents what Patty said when she saw the snake?
Ice cream.

What could happen if you ate too many desserts?
You could become piebald.

detectives
Name the most famous Arab detective.
The Seek of Araby.

What is a store detective called?
A counter spy.

diamonds
  Where is the largest diamond in New York kept?
  In the baseball field.

  Why do you have to have strong nerves to be a diamond-cutter?
  It takes courage to facet.

diatribe
  What is diatribe?
  What North American Indians used to do before going into battle.

dictionaries
  What should you do if you see your dog chewing this dictionary?
  Take the words right out of his mouth.

diet
  What is the staple diet of Russia?
  The reddish.

  What could you call someone who is a real artist at creating colorful diets?
  A diet Titian.

differences
  What is the difference between a new five-cent piece and an old-fashioned dime?
  Five cents.

  How much difference is there between the North Pole and the South Pole?
  All the difference in the world.

  What is the difference between a glass of iced water and a glass of soda?
  The price.

dimes
  What did the dime say when it got stuck in the slot?
  "Money's tight these days!"

dinosaurs
  How does one dinosaur tell another to hurry up?
  "Pronto, Sauras!"

diplomats
  Why is an eastern diplomat like a western baby?
  Because if he can't get attention he'll often Bangladesh.

disasters
  What disasters occur every twenty-four hours?
  Day breaks and night falls.

disguise

If you are going to rob a bank, what's the best disguise to wear?
Put on a stocking mask. Denier won't be recognized.

dishes

A riddle from Siberia:
There is a silver dish floating in the middle of the sea.
The sun.

divers

How does a diver get paid if he works extra hours?
Undertime.

division

Why did Chicago name one of its thoroughfares "Division Street"?
That's where all the optometrists have their offices.

divorce

Why did the comedian's wife sue for divorce?
She claimed he was trying to joke her to death.

Why is divorce like probation?
It's an early way out of an old institution.

Dobermans

Why did the Doberman pinscher?
Because her leash had expired.

docks

Hickory, dickory dock,
The mouse ran up the clock.
The clock struck one
And down it run.
Hickory, dickory dock.
The guillotine in action.*

---

* This charming example of an answer of Elizabethan-era complexity actually must have been created after 1789, the year that Dr. Guillotin first proposed the device. Here, dock has a double meaning. "The dock" is still used today as referring to the place in which a prisoner has his punishment meted out. And, of course, "to dock" still means to cut off. Hickory is a hard wood suitable for guillotine construction. Dickory has two relative meanings. The first is based on the old word "dicky" meaning shaky, referring to the impermanence of the structure. The more specific is that it also meant a trial. In this latter sense it only survives today in the verb "to dicker." "The mouse" is a colorful description of the blade, probably suggested by the way that it scurries down after its prey. (The use of an animal's name for an object is not unusual, e.g., the weasel in the spinning song "Pop Goes the Weasel.") "Ran up the clock," depicting the blade being raised, supplies an overtone of the critical moment approaching. "The clock struck one" is symbolically like the tolling of a funeral bell yet also predictive; certainly one (the victim) is about to be struck. The ambiguity of "And down it run" is deliberate. Not only has the clock run down, i.e., the victim's time is gone, but "the mouse" is on its way. The last line, "Hickory, dickory dock" thus becomes a logical conclusion when the verbal sense of dock is applied; the victim has been docked by the hickory dickory.

doctors

Why are doctors good-natured?
Because they don't mind if you stick out your tongue at them.

Who was the busiest doctor in the Bible?
Job. He had the most patience.

Why didn't Mother let the doctor operate on Father?
She didn't want anyone else to open her male.

Why do doctors make good sailors?
Because they are accustomed to see sickness.

dogma

What is meant by dogma?
A mother of pups.

dogs

How do you stop a dog from barking in the back seat of your car?
Put him in the front seat.

Why does a dog turn around three times before lying down?
Because one good turn deserves another.

How do you keep dogs out of the streets?
Put them in barking lots!

When is a sheep dog most likely to go into the house?
When the door is open.

You've heard of a flying fox, so what is a flying dog?
A Skye Terrier.

When is a black dog not a black dog?
When it's a greyhound.

Why does a dog wag his tail?
Because no one else will wag it for him.

What kind of dog has no tail?
A hot dog.

Why does a dog have so many friends?
Because he wags his tail instead of his tongue.

dollars

What is the fastest way to double your dollars?
Fold them.

donkeys

What is the difference between a donkey and a postage stamp?
One you lick with a stick and the other you stick with a lick.

What did the hungry donkey say when he only had thistles to eat?
"Thistle have to do."

There is a donkey on one side of a deep river, and a bundle of hay on the
other side. How can the donkey get the hay? There is no bridge, and he cannot
swim. Do you give up?
So did the other donkey.

doomsday

What is doomsday?
The last day of the weak.

doors

When is a door not a door?
When it is ajar.

What goes through a door but never goes in and never comes out?
A keyhole.

Three enter it by one door;
Each comes out his own.
A shirt.

A little house full of meat,
No door to go in and eat.
A nut.

doughnuts

Where were the first doughnuts fried?
In Greece.

How can five persons divide five doughnuts so that everyone gets one and one
is still left on the plate?
One person takes the plate with the doughnut.

dowager

What is a dowager?
One who bets on the New York Stock Exchange averages.

down

What goes down but can never come up?
A well.

Dracula

What was the great contribution that Dracula made to modern medicine?
He was the first blood count.

Which bank did Dracula break into?
The blood bank.

dragons

When a dragon is breathing fire, how can you calm him down?
Throw water at him and he will let off steam.

What did the mother of the twin dragons complain?
"I can hardly extinguish them apart!"

Why do dragons sleep during the day?
So they can fight knights.

drama

Who is America's most famous writer of folk dramas?
Drama Moses.

drama coaches

Why did the drama coach always start his lessons with a blast?
Because he was a tutor.

drawings

Why are the markings at Stonehenge like a caveman's drawings?
No one knows who druid.

Dresden

Dresden was formerly a type of lace. How is the word used today?
"My God, look at what she's dresden!"

dresses

What is the latest thing in dresses?
Nightdresses.

What kind of dress do you have but never wear?
Your address.

drilling

What did the wall say to the electric drill?
"You bore me."

What did the drill reply?
"I'm sorry. I'll be through soon."

drinking
What should a prizefighter drink?
Punch.

Who drinks in the king's cup and doesn't fear the king?
A fly.

driving
Can you drive a car over water?
Sure. If you can find a bridge.

How do you drive a baby buggy?
Tickle its feet.

drogue
The word "drogue" is familiar to parachutists but what did it originally mean?
An air force shoot-out, usually held outside a drogue store.

drugs
What is a female drug addict called when she saves somebody?
A heroine.

drums
When you listen to a drum, why are you like a fair judge?
Because you listen to both sides.

ducks
What did the mother duck say to her ducklings when it was time for dinner?
"Go jump in the lake!"

Why does a duck put its head under water?
For divers reasons.

Why does a duck bring its head out of the water?
For sundry reasons.

What was the first thing the eider duck told her daughter?
"If you want to line a nest, you really must get down to it."

What happened to the duck that flew upside down?
It quacked up.

What do you call a crate full of ducks?
A box of quackers.

dullness
What has the dullest life in the house?
A bed—it gets dressed every day but never goes out.

dying

What's the best place to go when you're dying?
Into the living room.

*Q. How can you fall from the **Empire State Building** and not get hurt?*

A. Fall from the front doorstep.

E

Why is *E* the unluckiest letter?
Because it is never in cash, always in debt, and never out of danger.

Do you know a word that starts with *E* and has only one letter in it?
Envelope.

eagles

Why did the eagle fly over the mountain?
Because it couldn't fly under it.

ears

Why should you never tell secrets in a cornfield?
Because the corn has ears.

What kind of ears does an engine have?
Engineers.

What did one ear say to the other?
"Meet you round the block."

What is big at the bottom, little at the top, and has ears?
A mountain. (You mean, you've never heard of mountaineers?)

earth
How far is it from earth to heaven?
As far as you can see.

ease
What is easy to get into but hard to get out of?
Trouble.

eating
What do you call a cow eating grass?
A lawn mooer.

If a girl ate her mother and her father, what would that make her?
An orphan.

What would you serve, but never want to eat?
A tennis ball.

Why do white sheep eat more than black sheep?
Because there are more of them.

What is brought to the table and cut but never eaten?
A deck of cards.

A riddle from India:
Eat and drink it can,
Walk it cannot.
A tree.

What do the elephants in the zoo at Cannes eat?
Canned elephant food.

As long as I eat, I live,
But when I drink, I die.
Fire.

What is the greatest feat in eating ever known?
There once was a man who commenced by bolting a door, after which he threw up a window, and then sat down and swallowed a whole story!

eavesdroppers
Name the world's best-known eavesdropper.
The icicle.

eaves troughs
What is the difference between an eaves trough and a poor baseball fielder?
One catches the drops and the other drops the catches.

Edison, Thomas

What happened to Thomas Edison one day in his laboratory?
He had a revolting experience.

eggs

How should you serve dinosaur eggs?
With hot mastodon.

What did the egg say to the electric mixer?
"I know when I'm beaten!"

If a rooster laid an egg on the top of the barn, which way would it roll?
Roosters don't roll.

How many eggs can you eat on an empty stomach?
Just one, because then your stomach won't be empty.

How would you divide ten eggs equally among seven people?
Scramble them.

Every morning the farmer had eggs for breakfast. He owned no chickens and he never got eggs from anyone else's chickens. Where did he get his eggs?
From his ducks.

Egypt

Why is a pleasure trip to Egypt only fit for the very old?
Because it's a see-Nile thing to do.

Eiffel Tower, the

Why is the most famous tower in Paris called the Eiffel?
Because it offers so many attractive views.

electricity

What happened to the discoverer of electricity?
He got a nasty shock.

elephants

Why is an elephant gray?
So you won't mistake him for a bluebird.

What time is it when an elephant sits on a fence?
Time to get a new fence.

Why do elephants hide behind trees?
To trip the ants.

If you want to ride an elephant, what's the first step?
You've got to learn howdah.

How do you get down from an elephant?
You don't. You get down from a duck.

Why is an elephant like a brick?
Because neither of them can climb a tree.

How do you fit six elephants in a car?
Three in the front seat and three in the back.

What is the difference between an elephant and a flea?
An elephant can have fleas but a flea can't have elephants.

Why does an elephant wear sunglasses?
If you were the one they were telling all these jokes about, you would want to hide, too!

elevators
Why do elevators run up and down?
They're in too much of a hurry to walk.

What did one elevator say to the other?
"I think I'm coming down with something."

Elijah
Why must Elijah's parents have been good business people?
Well, at least between them they made a prophet!

emblems
Why is the emblem of the United States more lasting than that of France, England, Ireland, or Scotland?
The lily may fade and its leaves decay,
The rose from its stem may sever,
The shamrock and thistle may pass away,
But the stars will shine forever.

Empire State Building, the
How can you fall from the Empire State Building and not get hurt?
Fall from the front doorstep.

employees
Why are union employees like dogs with broken tails?
They both have their weekends.

Why are so many people reluctant to become employees in the garment industry?
It's a seamy business.

emptiness
What's empty in the daytime and full at night?
A bed.

end
What do you find at the end of everything?
The letter G.

engineers
Why do people with little imagination make the best railway engineers?
Because they have one-track minds.

engines
Why is a railway engine like a child that misbehaves a great deal?
It often has a tender behind.

What do steam engines eat?
Coal cuts.

England
What do people in England call little black cats?
Kittens.

envelopes
What did the envelope say when it was licked?
It shut up and said nothing.

escape
If you were locked in a room with nothing but a baseball bat, how would you get out?
Take three strikes.

Eskimos
How would you define the Eskimos as a race?
God's frozen people.

If an Eskimo mother had a boy and a girl, what would they be?
Blubber and sister.

What did the Eskimo say after his neighbor had finished building his igloo?
"That's an ice house you have!"

What happened when the Eskimo girl fell out with her boyfriend?
She gave him the cold shoulder.

What do they sing at an Eskimo's coming-out party?
"Freeze a jolly good fellow!"

eternity
Why is eternity like a circle?
It has neither beginning nor end.

What is that which is
The beginning of eternity,

The end of time and space,
The beginning of every end,
The end of every race?
The letter E.

Eve
What did Eve do when she wanted sugar?
She raised Cain.

evening
From Turkey, this puzzler:
In the evening I looked—
There it was.
In the morning I looked—
It was gone.
Darkness.

everyone
What is it that everyone has at the same time?
A name.

everything
What is everything doing at the same time?
Growing older.

explosives
What happened to the anarchist who thought he had invented a new explosive?
He bombed out.

eyes
A riddle, a riddle, as I suppose,
A hundred eyes, and never a nose.
A bag of potatoes.

A riddle, a riddle, as I suppose,
A *thousand* eyes and never a nose.
A sieve.

When are your eyes not your eyes?
When the wind makes them water.

What did one eye say to the other?
"Just between you and me, there is something that smells."

The boy with a hundred eyes behind?
A peacock.

What always has one eye open but cannot see?
A needle.

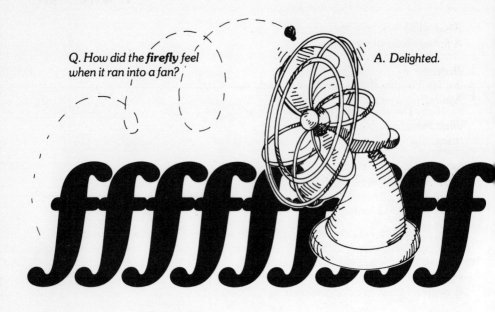

*Q. How did the **firefly** feel when it ran into a fan?*

A. Delighted.

F

Why is the letter *F* like a cow's tail?
Because it is the end of beef.

Why does the letter *F* end summer?
Because it makes all fall.

faces

What is the cheapest feature of the face?
Nostrils—two for a scent.

What has a face but no head, hands but no feet, yet travels everywhere and is usually running?
A watch.

factory

Why did the elephants quit the factory?
They got tired of working for peanuts.

fairies

What is the nicest thing about being a fairy queen?
You can have anything you wand.

fairs

Why is a church fair like making love on the midway?
It's a bazaar experience.

What is the best kind of agricultural fair?
A farmer's daughter.

falling

If a fat man fell downstairs, what would he fall against?
Against his wishes.

What falls often but never gets hurt?
Raindrops.

fans

Why did the cat sleep with the fan on?
He wanted to be a cool cat.

far

What should parents do if they feel that their daughter is going too far?
Give her a brake.

How far is it from one end of the earth to the other?
A day's journey. (The sun does it in a day.)

fare

What is the worst kind of fare for a person to live on?
Warfare.

farmers

Why is a farmer using a plow like a steamship in midocean?
Because one sees the plow while the other plows the sea.

When is a farmer mean?
When he pulls the ears off the corn.

Why were the farmers so happy when the price of pork shot up?
It created a gold mine in the sty.

What is the difference between a farmer and a seamstress?
One gathers what he sows and the other sews what she gathers.

Why is a gentleman farmer like a former hero?
He has effete of clay.

Why did the farmer run the steamroller over his fields?
He wanted to raise mashed potatoes.

Why is a rich farmer like a man with bad teeth?
Because he has a good many acres.

What is the difference between a farmer and an actor?
One minds his peas and the other his cues.

fashions

What is always at the head of fashion yet always out of date?
The letter F.

fast

Who are the fastest people on earth?
The Russians.

What often checks a fast man?
A bridal.

fastening

What fastens two people together yet touches only one?
A wedding ring.

fat

What is the best way to get fat?
Go to the butcher shop.

Why do fat people usually seem happy?
They try not to end their conversations with size.

Who is Mexico's most famous fat man?
Pauncho Villa.

fathers

Besides Adam, who in the Bible had no father?
Joshua. He was the son of Nun.

There is a father with twice six sons; each son has thirty daughters each with one cheek white and the other black. They never see each other's faces nor live more than twenty-four hours. What is this old riddle describing?
The year and its parts.

What do the Scots call a father goose?
A mongoose.

feathers

What is lighter than a feather but can be bigger than a giant?
A giant's shadow.

What is it that you can't hold for five minutes yet it's as light as a feather?
Your breath.

feeling

What is it that has never been felt,
Never been seen, never been heard,

Never existed,
And still has a name?
Nothing.

What do you have when you don't feel well?
You probably have gloves on.

feet

Four feet sat on four feet,
Waiting for four feet.
A cat sat on a chair, waiting for a mouse.

What has no feet but always wears shoes?
The sidewalk.

Why do elephants have flat feet?
From jumping out of palm trees.

What has feet and legs and nothing else?
Stockings.

fences

Why do they put fences around graveyards?
Because so many people are dying to get in.

A little white fence that's always wet,
But never rained on yet.
Teeth.

Five copycats were sitting on a fence. One jumped off. How many were left?
None. They were all copycats.

Which kind of lawyer should a fence send for?
Defense lawyer.

fencing

What happened when the fencing team tried to wrap up the tournament?
They kept getting foiled.

fields

What goes all over the field and leaves a white cap on every stump?
Snow.

In Russia, they pose this one:
The field cannot be measured; the sheep cannot be counted;
the shepherd has two horns.
The sky, stars, and moon.

When is a straight field not a straight field?
When it is a rye field.

I came to a field and couldn't get through it;
So I took a course and learned how to do it.
Fence.

fighting

Two men heard about the same job. Both men wanted it. They fought and killed each other. Who got the job?
The undertaker.

filibusters

Why did the southern senators start a filibuster?
They thought it was time to throw their wait around.

filleting

If you are asked to fillet fish, what should you do?
Don't make any bones about it.

filling

If ten men can fill a thousand-gallon tank in ten hours, how long would it take for ten men to fill a ten-gallon tank?
You can't get ten men into a ten-gallon tank!

fingers

Why are a giant's fingers always eleven inches long?
If they were an inch longer each would be a foot.

What has hands but no fingers?
A clock.

Four fingers and a thumb,
Yet flesh and bone have I none.
A glove.

Finland

Why would a revolution in Finland be extremely dangerous?
Because it would be a fight to the Finnish.

fire

What is the best way to make a fire with two sticks?
Make sure one of the sticks is a match.

What is the best way to fire an arrow?
Light the tip.

firecrackers
What did the big firecracker say to the little firecracker?
"My pop is bigger than your pop."

Why do firecrackers hate rain?
They don't like sodden surprises.

fire-eaters
Why did the fire-eater make the front pages?
His flame had spread.

fireflies
How did the firefly feel when it ran into a fan?
Delighted.

firemen
What is the difference between a fireman and a nightclub bouncer?
One soaks the fires and the other fires the soaks.

Complete the statement "She was only a fireman's daughter—" *
Choose one: A. *"—but she was a lusty quench."*
              B. *"—but she knew how to get new hose."*
              C. *"—but she sure could put out your fire!"*

fish
Why are fish so smart?
Because they travel in schools.

How do little fish make a living?
They start on a very small scale.

What kind of fish do you find in a bird cage?
Perch.

What fish is very musical?
A piano-tuna.

fishermen
What is the difference between a fisherman and a lazy student?
One baits his hook and the other hates his book.

Why should a commercial fisherman be wealthy?
Because his business is all net profit.

---

* Because it is questionable whether this structure is truly a riddle, we only give this one example. Many others exist. Some tend to do damage to the reputations of the daughters of farmers, fishermen, etc. We hope that our picking on the firemen's daughters will not cause them to be two-alarmed!

What do the Swedish people call their government's assistance to fishermen?
Herring aids.

fishing

Why are so many people mad about fishing?
Because it's an easy thing to get hooked on.

Why do so many people like to go deep-sea fishing?
They have sailfish motives.

flannel

Why did Mrs. Murphy call her son "Flannel"?
Because he shrank from washing.

fleas

Why was the mother flea crying?
Because all of her children had gone to the dogs.

How did the father flea get home for Christmas?
By Greyhound.

What did the dog say to the flea?
"Don't bug me!"

What happens to a flea when it becomes really angry?
It gets hopping mad.

What did the boy flea say to the girl flea when they came out of the movies?
"Shall we walk home or take a dog?"

flies

What has eighteen legs and catches flies?
A baseball team.

What has two holes and flies?
An outhouse.

What has five holes and flies?
An outhouse for quintuplets.

floating

What floats on the water light as can be,
Yet thousands of people cannot lift it free?
A bubble.

How do you make an elephant float?
You take a medium-sized elephant and add two scoops of ice cream and some root beer.

flowers

Why did the busy bee call the flowers lazy?
Because they were always in bed.

Various animals and plants are being sent into space for experiments but what one flower will never be used?
A space-age traveler the cosmos not.

Why was the florist suspicious of the flowers?
Because they were discovered in a garden plot.

A dish full of all kinds of flowers:
Can you guess this riddle? I'll give you two hours!
Honey.

flying

What flies forever
And rests never?
The wind.

What flies around the house and leaves a white glove on the window sill?
Snow.

What always remains down even when it flies up in the air?
A feather.

What is it that is wingless and legless, yet flies and cannot be imprisoned?
Your voice.

Why should you avoid traveling by flying carpet?
It's a rugged experience.

focus

Why did the Texas widow call her ranch "Focus"?
Because it's where the sons raise meat.

font

In printing, what is "font"?
Type that was formerly lost.

foods

What food suggests green tarts?
Pickles.

What food is moon material?
Cheese.

What food keeps the labor unions strong?
Beef.

What food is impertinent?
Sauce.

What food represents dirt and goblins?
Sandwiches.

What food represents a taxi and a period of time?
Cabbage.

What food represents what the patient has and what the doctor gets?
Coffee.

foot
What can be only eight inches long and three inches wide yet hold a whole foot?
A shoe.

football
Why is Rugby football like a loaf of bread?
Because of its scrums.

football players
What's the difference between a good football player and an industrious business person?
One times his passes well and the other passes his time well.

Why are first-class footballers like accomplished musicians?
Because they are very good players.

If a football player smuggles his girlfriend into the dressing room, what should he do with her while the game is on?
Locker up.

Frankenstein
How did Baron von Frankenstein overcome his loneliness?
He learned to make friends.

Franklin, Benjamin
What did Benjamin Franklin say when he discovered electricity in the clouds?
Nothing. He was too shocked.

French
How can you tell a true Frenchman?
When it comes time to eat, they are real messrs.

Freud
What is a Freudian slip?
A garment designed to be worn under a see-through blouse.

friends
Who is your greatest friend?
Your nose, because it will run for you till it drops.

As I went walking up a lane,
I met a friend who knows no pain.
I knocked off his head and sucked his blood
And left him standing there, a dud.
A bottle of wine.

frogs
What did the bad frog say to the good frog?
"I hope you croak!"

Whom does a frog call when she wants to get her eyes checked?
A hoptician.

fruit
What unripe fruit do newlyweds resemble?
A green pear.

fullness
You can have a house full, a yard full,
But you can't catch a bowl full!
Smoke, air, fog, or mist.

What's full in the daytime and empty at night?
A pair of shoes.

fun
If you're looking for fun on the farm, why should you try standing behind a mule?
You might get a kick out of it.

funerals
What is another name for a funeral?
A coffin spell.

furs
What fur did Adam and Eve wear?
Bareskin.

Why could an expensive fur coat sometimes remind you of a person in need of psychiatric treatment?
Because one may be of a minky kind and the other of a kinky mind.

Q. What do you call someone who gets all excited watching **games** on television?

A. A chairleader.

G
Why is the letter G like the sun?
Because it is the center of light.

games
What is the quietest game in the world?
Bowling—you can hear a pin drop.

What game do judges play well?
Tennis—because it's played in court.

What do you call someone who gets all excited watching games on television?
A chairleader.

gardeners
When is a gardener like a mystery writer?
When he digs up a plot.

What do most gardeners not like to grow?
Old.

gardens
What is the first thing you put in a garden?
Your foot.

gargoyles
What is a gargoyle?
Something you wash your throat with when it's sore.

gas
What is a ten-letter word that starts with gas?
Automobile.

gates
What gates are like church bells?
Toll gates.

geese
Why is a goose like an icicle?
Because it grows down.

In Wales, the gypsies pose this one:
There is a great field full of geese and one gander.
The sky, stars, and moon.

geometry
What geometric figure is like a lost parrot?
A polygon.

getting
I went to the wood and got it.
I sat me down and looked at it.
The more I looked, the less I liked it.
Against my will I brought it home
Because I couldn't help it.
A thorn or splinter.

ghosts
Why are ghosts very simple things?
Because they can easily be seen through.

What did Mother Ghost say to Baby Ghost when they got in the car?
"Fasten your sheet belt."

What did Baby Ghost say to Mother Ghost?
"Do you believe in people?"

What did Mother Ghost reply to Baby Ghost?
"Don't spook unless you are spooken to."

What did Baby Ghost say to Bully Ghost?
"Leave me alone or I'll tell my mummy."

What do ghosts have for breakfast?
Ghost Toasties and evaporated milk.

What do ghosts eat for lunch?
Boo loney sandwiches.

What do ghosts have for dinner?
Ghoulash.

giants

How do you spell blind giant?
Blnd gant. You spell it that way because a blind giant has no eyes.

giraffes

Why are giraffes' necks so long?
Because their heads are a long way from their bodies.

What are the five animals in the giraffe family?
The mother giraffe, the father giraffe, and the three baby giraffes.

Why does a giraffe need so little to eat?
Because it makes a little go a long way.

girls

What is the difference between a girl and a postage stamp?
One is a female and the other is a mail fee.

How many pretty girls all in a straight line would it take to reach from Boston to New York if the distance is 230 miles?
Two hundred and thirty, because a miss is as good as a mile.

When does a girl lose her self-possession?
When she gives herself away.

Where do bad girls go?
Most everywhere.

Why do girls make good army volunteers?
Because they are accustomed to bare arms.

What is the principal difference between thin girls and fat girls?
Thin girls may love their men passively but fat girls buxom.

giving

What two things can you give away and still keep?
Your word and a cold.

glasses

What do you call a fish that wears glasses?
A spectacled trout.

I dropped a full glass and didn't spill a drop of water. Why?
Because the glass was full of milk.

glazing

What is double glazing?
A man with glasses who has had too much to drink.

goats

Why is it hard to talk when there is a goat around?
Because he always butts in.

Why are goats so easy to fool?
Because they will swallow anything.

goblins

Why did the goblin quit the game?
Because it didn't have a ghost of a chance.

Godiva, Lady

What did Lady Godiva say to her sister before she took off for her famous ride?
"Bare with me."

What happened to Lady Godiva's horse when he saw that she had no clothes on?
It made him shy.

going

What goes up and down and around inside the house and then sits in a closet and waits?
A broom.

gold

If a king sits on gold, who sits on silver?
The Lone Ranger.

Golden Gate Bridge, the

Why is the Golden Gate Bridge like a teacher in trouble?
Because it has been suspended.

golf

Why did the boy at the golf course get promoted?
He isn't the caddie used to be.

Why is a golf course like a Gruyère cheese?
Because they both have holes in them.

Why does a man become a golf pro?
In order to earn his bread and putter.

golfer

Why did the golfer bring an extra pair of pants with him?
In case he got a hole-in-one!

Why are golfers like cavemen?
Because they always walk around with clubs in their hands.

gorillas

Where does a two-ton gorilla sit when he goes to the movies?
Anywhere he wants to!

gout

Why is gout like reciprocated love?
Because it is a joint affection.

government

What is the best thing to ensure stable government?
A strong mare.

graffiti

What should you do if you feel strongly about graffiti?
Sign a partition.

grammar

What part of speech is kissing?
A conjunction.

Which is better, "a house burned down" or "a house burned up"?
Neither. Both are very bad.

granny

What is the difference between your granny and your granary?
One is your born kin and the other your corn bin.

grapes

What did the grape say when it was stepped on by an elephant?
Nothing . . . it just gave a little wine.

grass

First you see me in the grass
Dressed in yellow gay,
Next I am in dainty white,
Then I fly away.
A dandelion.

How do you spell "dried grass" in three letters?
Hay.

grasshoppers
Why do the Japanese eat grasshoppers?
It's a locust food.

graveyards
On which side of a country church is the graveyard always situated?
On the outside.

gravity
What sentence would you get if you broke the law of gravity?
A suspended sentence.

gray
What is gray, has four legs, and a trunk?
A mouse going on vacation.

greatness
The greater it is, the less it can be seen. What is it?
Darkness.

greed
Why is greed like bad memory?
Because it is always for getting.

green
Once it was green and growing,
Now it is dead and singing.
A violin.

greenhouse
Why did the greenhouse call the doctor?
It had window pains.

ground
What did the ground say to the rain?
"If you keep that up, my name will be mud."

groundhog
What is a groundhog?
A big sausage.

Guinevere, Lady
Why did Lady Guinevere want a night off?
Because he had his armor round her.

What did Lady Guinevere say when she first met King Arthur?
"Arthur any more at home like you?"

guitars

Why is a guitar like a turkey being made ready for the oven?
They both have to be plucked.

What happened when the electric guitar was plugged into the lamp?
It played light music.

Why wouldn't Ralph's guitar work?
Because it only knew how to play.

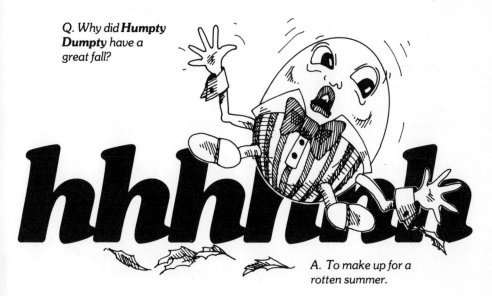

*Q. Why did **Humpty Dumpty** have a great fall?*

A. To make up for a rotten summer.

H

Why is the letter *H* the one a deaf woman would most like to have?
Because it would make her ear hear.

haggis

In Scotland, haggis is a traditional banquet dish. They usually have a bagpiper pipe it in. What do they use if they can't afford a bagpiper?
A plumber.

What do you know about a Scotsman who claims that he eats haggis for dessert every night?
He is just pudding you on.

haiku

Where does the haiku come from?
A soprano pigeon.

hair

Three men were in a boat that capsized. Why did only two of them get their hair wet?
One was bald.

Why does the aging movie star feel so sad every time he gets his hair done?
Because his favorite barber dyes.

haircuts

Where does a sheep get his hair cut?
At the baa-baa shop.

Why is the price of haircuts causing so much concern today?
It is becoming shear nonsense.

ham

When the ham lover fell ill what did his doctor tell him?
"Perhaps your trichinosis was infatuate."

hamburger

How do you make a hamburger for an elephant?
First you get a big bun . . .

If you hold a hamburger horizontally, which side of it is the left side?
The part that isn't eaten.

hammer

Why does a cowboy take a hammer to bed?
So that he can hit the hay.

What is the motto of the Hammer Manufacturers' Association?
"The nails must get through."

handcuffs

Why are handcuffs like souvenirs?
They are made for two wrists.

If handcuffs cuff hands what do pantcuffs cuff?
Prisoners who are out of breath.

hands

What did the big hand say to the little hand?
"Got a minute?"

What did the little hand say to the big hand?
"I'll be back in an hour."

Which hand should you use to stir stew?
Neither. Use a spoon!

Why is your hand like a hardware store?
Because it has nails.

Why are hands like Miami?
They wouldn't be the same without the palms.

hanging

What is one thing in the world you can't hang on a nail?
An egg.

You can hang me on the wall, but if you take me down, you cannot hang me up again.
Wallpaper.

happiness

What is the secret of happiness for a woman over forty?
Not to worry about the menopause but the men who don't.

If happiness is a two-way street, what is dating a stranger?
A blind dally.

harps

Why do so few people decide to learn harp playing?
It takes a lot of pluck.

What did the harp say to the violin?
"I'd be harpy if you'd string along."

hats

Why is a hat like a king?
It has a crown.

What are hats for?
To cover the area head.

If you drop your hat into the Black Sea, what will it become?
Wet.

What's the answer to this riddle from Haiti? Big shot's hat fell off but he can't pick it up.
A palm tree.

When is a hat not a hat?
When it becomes a woman.

having

You don't have it, you don't want it, but if you did have it, you wouldn't take a million dollars for it.
A bald head.

What is it everyone would like to have yet wants to get rid of right away?
A good appetite.

Luke had it first, Paul had it last; boys never have it; girls have it but once; Maureen O'Sullivan had it twice in the same place, but when she married Patrick O'Brien she never had it again.
The letter L.

hay

Why do farmers store hay in barns?
So that when winter comes they'll be fodder ahead.

A farmer had 2½ stacks of hay in one row and 3½ stacks in another row. How many haystacks did he have when he put them together?
One.

Why did the man take hay to bed with him?
He wanted to feed his nightmare.

What do you get when you cross an octopus with a pile of hay?
Eight straw brooms.

headlines

What headlines do women like least?
Wrinkles.

heads

What has a head but can't think?
A ship.

What has twenty heads but can't think?
A book of matches.

What has a head and a tail but no body?
A coin.

What has one head, one foot, one body, four legs?
A bed.

What has two heads and one body?
A barrel or a rolling pin or a drum.

Who always thinks that two heads are better than one?
A barber.

Riddle me, riddle me, what is that
Over the head and under the hat?
Hair.

Sometimes with a head,
Sometimes with no head at all,
Sometimes with a tail,
Sometimes with no tail at all.
What am I?
A wig.

What is lower with a head than without it?
A pillow.

Green head,
Yellow toes,
If you don't tell me this riddle,
I'll wring your nose!
A duck.

What grows head down and feet up?
An onion.

health

Why does Katie always get *B*'s in Health?
Because she has hives.

Who always enjoys poor health?
The doctor.

hearing

What is it we hear when it is born but never hear after it is born?
A noise.

What has ears and can't hear?
Corn.

You can hear me.
You can see what I do.
Me, you cannot see.
The wind.

hearses

What makes the hearse horse?
The coffin.

heartburn

Why did the condemned man have heartburn?
It must have been something the assassinate.

hearts

What is it that's got a heart in its head?
Lettuce.

Why is the heart of a woman like the moon?
Because it changes continually but there is always a man in it.

Which English king must have had a heart transplant?
*Richard the First, because when he became a Crusader his followers claimed
that he had the heart of a lion.*

heat

Which is faster, heat or cold?
Heat—you can always catch cold.

Why is heating a house like having the flu?
It is hard to keep warm if you have a bad coal.

What stays hot even when it's in the refrigerator?
Mustard.

heaven

What kind of men go to heaven?
Dead men.

Why are there no bearded men in heaven?
Because men get in by a close shave.

Henry the Eighth

Why did Henry the Eighth have so many wives?
He liked to marry in haste and repeat at leisure.

hens

Why does a hen lay eggs?
Because if she lets them drop, they will break.

What do you call a hen who is afraid to cross the road?
A chicken.

Why does a lighthouse keeper raise hens?
So that he will have beacon and eggs.　,

Which side of a hen has the most feathers?
The outside.

Why is a black hen smarter than a white one?
Because a black hen can lay a white egg but a white hen can't lay a black egg.

herbs

Which herb is most injurious to beauty?
Thyme.

Hercules

Why was Hercules discouraged when he was told to clean the Augean Stables?
He was faced with an offal problem.

here

What is the difference between here and there?
The letter T.

heroines
What was the heroine of the Irish Industrial Revolution called?
Spinning Jenny.

herrings
Why is a herring like a graveyard?
Because it is full of bones.

Why should you never offer a herring a drink?
You could end up with pickled herring.

high
High as a house,
Low as a mouse,
Bitter as gall,
Sweet after all.
A walnut: the tree (high), the nut (small or low), the hull (bitter), the meat (sweet).

highways
What do you call someone who has studied highway construction?
A roads scholar.

What did the highway say to the road?
"Do you ever get that run-down feeling?"

hills
What is the difference between a hill and a pill?
A hill is hard to get up and a pill is hard to get down.

Why is a hill like a lazy dog?
Because it is a slope up.

hindsight
What is hindsight?
Watching the can-can.

hinges
Why are girls like hinges?
Because they are things to adore.

hippopotamuses
Where do you find hippopotamuses?
It depends on where you left them!

Why does a hippopotamus have red toenails?
So that he can hide in a cherry tree.

What was the hippopotamus doing on the highway?
About two miles an hour.

historians
What is the historian's favorite fruit?
Dates.

Why is it frustrating to be a historian?
You keep going around in circas.

history
What is a history of cars called?
An autobiography.

Hitler
What did Hitler mutter after he captured the French military equipment?
"Is this all the tanks I get?"

hives
What song are you most likely to hear by a hive?
"Bee It Ever So Humble, There's No Place Like Comb!"

hobbies
Why is keeping birds an economical hobby?
An aviary is a cheep place.

hoboes
What would you call a hobo jungle after a rainstorm?
A damp tramp camp.

hockey
What's the hardest thing about learning to play hockey?
The ice!

hogs
Why is a wild hog like an aristocrat?
They both depend on their roots.

holes
If you crawled into a hole dug clear through the earth, where would you come out?
Out of the hole.

What is full of holes and holds water?
A sponge.

How much earth is there in a hole three feet deep by six feet?
None.

What pierces and leaves no hole?
Sound.

Two men dug a hole in five days. How many days would it have taken them to dig half a hole?
You can't dig half a hole.

Would you rather go hungry or have seven holes in your head?
You already have seven holes in your head.

How can you use the holes left over from making doughnuts?
Tie them together with string to make fishnets.

Holland
Why should we not believe one word that comes from Holland?
Because it is such a low-lying country.

Hollywood
Why is Hollywood a good place to hire singers?
You can get them by the choir.

Holy Mother, the
What did the Holy Mother say when confronted with the manger?
"If you expect me to have the baby in that thing, I'll have to go on a crèche diet!"

homes
Why do so many people have birds in their homes?
Because they make tweet music.

What did the railroad worker's daughter do when she got tired of being tied down at home?
She made tracks for a better station in life.

honey
Why is hunting for honey like a legacy?
It is a bequest.

honeymoon
What is the basic drawback to a camping honeymoon?
It is apt to keep you two intent.

hopping
What's white outside, green inside, and hops?
A grasshopper sandwich.

horns
What has two horns when very young,

No horns in middle age,
And again two horns when old?
The moon.

horror

Why did Boris Karloff make so many horror movies?
He was successful beyond his wildest screams.

horses

What is the principal part of a horse?
The mane part.

Where does a horse hide?
Wither are whipple trees.

What did one horse say to the other?
"I can't remember your mane but your pace is familiar."

Why does a horse have six legs?
Because he has forelegs at the front and two at the back.

Why is it bad to have a horse that is too polite?
Everytime you come to a fence, it will let you go over first.

As they see it in Iran:
Two horses, white and black, chase each other forever in vain.
Day and night.

Why is a wild horse like an egg?
Because it must be broken before it can be used.

Why is a sick horse like a bad play?
Because it's not drawing any more and has to stop running.

What sort of horse can you put your shirt on and be sure you'll get it back?
A clothes horse.

Thirty-two white horses upon a red hill,
Now they tramp,
Now they champ,
Now they stand still.
Teeth and gums.

Why is a horse like a ball game?
Because it gets stopped by the rein.

hospitals

How do you qualify for work in a hospital?
By learning to carry a bedpan in an orderly fashion.

How could the hospital tell that Uncle Oscar was feeling better?
He began going from bed to nurse.

houses

If there is a red house on the right and a blue house on the left, where is the White House?
In Washington, D.C.

Why should you build your house in a ball field?
Because every house needs a base.

What is neither in the house, nor out of the house, but is still part of the house?
A window.

Why was the house empty?
The fire had gone out, the eggs had scrambled, the cards had cut, the rope had skipped, and the stockings had run.

As big as a house but lighter than a feather. What is it?
The shadow of a house.

In Burma, they ask:
What is like a beautiful house with twelve rooms? There are usually thirty people in each room. There are four doors left open. You have passed through these doors.
The house is the year; the twelve rooms are the months. The four doors lead to spring, summer, fall, and winter.

What's the one thing you need to do if you want to make an overall improvement in a house?
Put on a new roof.

On the hill there is a green house,
And in the green house there's a white house,
And in the white house there's a red house,
And in the red house
There are a lot of little black and white babies.
A watermelon.

When is a house not a house?
When it's afire.

hummingbirds

Why does a hummingbird hum?
Because it doesn't know the words.

humor

What do we mean by an incisive humorist?
One who always goes for the jocular vein.

Humpty Dumpty
Humpty Dumpty sat on a wall,
Humpty Dumpty had a great fall,
All the king's horses and all the king's men
Couldn't put Humpty Dumpty together again.
An egg. (Also said to refer to Charles I.)

Why *did* Humpty Dumpty have a great fall?
To make up for a rotten summer.

They say that Humpty Dumpty was a good egg until he cracked up—but what actually happened?
He made a crash move.

hunchbacks
Why did everyone feel sorry for the Hunchback of Notre Dame?
They hated to see his head go to waist.

hunger
What is the difference between a hungry person and a greedy person?
One longs to eat and the other eats too long.

hunters
What is the motto of the northern hunters?
"None but the brave deserves the bear."

hunting
I went hunting in the wood,
And those that I found and killed I left behind,
And those that I could not find
I brought home with me.
Fleas.

hurrying
What is the best thing to do in a hurry?
Nothing.

hurting
What can overpower a wrestler without hurting him?
Sleep.

What falls but never gets hurt?
Snow.

husbands
Why did the henpecked husband finally buy a robot?
So that when there was housework to do he could get out his robot and go fishing.

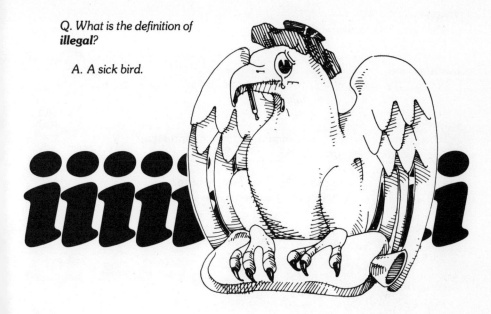

Q. What is the definition of **illegal**?

A. A sick bird.

I

Why is *I* the luckiest of the vowels?
Because it's the center of bliss, while E is in hell, and all the rest are in purgatory.

Why does this letter seem to frighten people?
We don't know, but it certainly makes your pal pail!

Icarus

After he failed to fly on his own, why was Icarus unpopular?
He was a soar loser.

icebergs

What is the difference between an iceberg and a clothes brush?
One crushes boats and the other brushes coats.

ice cream

Why is an ice cream cone like a race horse?
Because the more you lick it the faster it goes.

Idaho

What did Idaho?
I don't know, but Alaska.

ideas

When is an original idea like a clock?
When it strikes one.

illegal

What is the definition of illegal?
A sick bird.

immigration

Why did the immigration official let the pretty girl into the country?
Because she had two naturalize.

impressions

When can you be sure of making a good first impression?
When you lie down on the bed.

How can you be sure of making a bad impression?
By stepping in your neighbor's fresh concrete.

income tax

Why do income tax inspectors only work a six-day week?
It isn't legal to ransack business on Sunday.

incongruity

What's incongruous?
Where U.S. laws are made.

Industrial Revolution, the

What was the cause of the Industrial Revolution?
The workers weren't having jenny fun.

What was the first major result of the Industrial Revolution in Ireland?
The development of the mead-packing industry.

inflation

What was the first cause of inflation?
The invention of the balloon.

inhibitions

What is the basic problem with being inhibited?
You're all tied up in nots.

ink

What did one drop of ink ask the other drop of ink?
"Are all your relatives in the pen too?"

insects

What insect goes skin diving?
A mosquito.

intelligence

What animal has the highest level of intelligence?
The giraffe.

inventions
What kind of invention was the clock?
A timely one.

Why was the invention of the doorbell important?
It was of great help to the knock need.

inventors
How did its inventor discover gunpowder?
It came to him in a flash.

What do you call a great inventor's list of achievements?
His inventory.

What motive did the inventor of railroads have in view?
A locomotive.

investment
Why is going into the priesthood a good investment?
You can be sure of a surplice.

What is the poorest investment a farmer could make?
Buying a cow in a bull market.

invisibility
Why is the word "invisibility" such a strange one for its purpose?
It has five i's.

What is invisible yet can always be seen?
Visible.

Ireland
If Ireland could sink, what would still float?
Cork.

What does one and one make in Ireland?
An Irish stew.

Why is Ireland like a reform school?
We all hope that someday the people there will see the Eire of their ways.

iron
When is iron ironical?
When it is railing.

Why did Katie iron her four-leaf clover?
She wanted to press her luck.

islands

What islands are good to eat?
The Sandwich Islands.

If an island has islanders, what does a highland have?
Bagpipes.

*Q. What was it that drove Dr. **Jekyll** to his famous extremes?*

A. He was annoyed by people who kept getting under his Hyde.

J
Why is *J* the most active letter in the alphabet?
I'll tell you in a minute. I'm busy watching a blue J.

Jackson, Stonewall
What was the great advantage to the United States when it elected Stonewall Jackson?
It got a boulder president.

jailers
What is the difference between a jailer and a jeweler?
One sells watches and the other watches cells.

jails
Why is jail like marriage?
They are both institutions from which it is hard to escape.

jams
What makes a traffic jam?
A jar here, a jar there . . .

jealousy
What two letters spell a word meaning jealousy?
N V.

jeans
How did the fad of wearing jeans develop?
Young people liked the overall effect.

Jekyll, Dr.

What was it that drove Dr. Jekyll to his famous extremes?
He was annoyed by people who kept getting under his Hyde.

jesters

What did the jester have for dinner?
Fish and quips.

How did the court jester explain why he took the job?
"Jester survive!"

jets

How have jets changed the world?
They have made it go plane crazy.

jewelers

Why is a jeweler like a screeching singer?
Because he pierces the ears.

What did the thirsty jeweler say?
"I could lapidary."

Why is an overstocked jeweler like a prisoner in solitary confinement?
Because he has too much time on his hands.

jewels

What is the biggest jewel in the world?
A baseball diamond.

What does it mean when a belly dancer has a jewel in her navel?
She has just had a navel engagement.

Joan of Arc

What was Joan of Arc made of?
Maid of Orleans.

jobs

What is the most boring job in the world?
Being a termite inspector.

What is a put-up job?
The paper on the wall.

jockeys

Why is a jockey about to get off his horse like someone driving toward a lamppost?
He is going to alight.

What do you have to do if you want a job as a jockey?
You have to weight for it.

John, Saint
The Bible tells us that Saint John had what some would call a nightmare. What did he say first when he woke up?
"Armageddon out of here!"

jokes
What tree is like an old joke?
The chestnut.

If someone were to publish all the jokes in the United States, what could the book be called?
The Mirth of a Nation.

Why don't jokes last as long as church bells?
Because after they have been told a few times they are worn out.

When does a joke become a father?
When the punch line becomes apparent.

Why is a bad joke like an unsharpened pencil?
Because it has no point.

Jonah
Why is the story of Jonah and the whale so encouraging?
Because Jonah was down in the mouth but came out all right.

joys
I am part of joys and sorrows and home would not be home without me.
The letter O.

judges
What did the judge say when the skunk walked into the courtroom?
"Odor in the court!"

What did the judge say to his dentist?
"Do you swear to pull the tooth, the whole tooth, and nothing but the tooth?"

What did the judge say after he had finished work?
"It's been another trying day!"

What did the cooking-contest judge say when he became ill?
"It must have been something I rate."

jumpers
Why is a good-tempered horse not likely to be a good jumper?
Because it won't easily take offense.

In gymnastics, why does a jumper wear shorts?
To keep from being arrested.

jumping

What runs and jumps,
Stops and humps
And feels at home
In bramble clumps?
A rabbit.

Paul Bunyan used to go up to the tallest trees in all America, take off his boots and jump over them. How was he able to do this?
He didn't have very high boots.

Why does a Mexican jumping bean jump?
You would too, if you had been raised on that water!

jungles

What is the jungle commandment?
Honor thy parrots.

In the middle of the jungle stands an umbrella.
The mushroom.

How can you track an elephant in the jungle?
By the smell of peanuts on its breath.

Why should you never go into the jungle between two and four o'clock in the morning?
That's when the elephants come jumping out of the trees.

Why are so many jungle people pygmies?
Those are the ones that went into the jungle between two and four o'clock.

*Q. What is the difference between a **king**'s son, a monkey's mother, a bald head, and an orphan?*

A. A king's son is the heir-apparent; a monkey's mother is a hairy parent; a bald head has no hair apparent; and an orphan has nary a parent.

K
Why is the letter *K* like flour?
You can't make cake without it.

Why is it like a pig's tail?
Because it's the end of pork.

kaleidoscope
What is a kaleidoscope?
A device for watching automobile accidents.

kangaroos
Why was 1980 named "The Year of the Kangaroo"?
Because it was a leap year.

What did the mother kangaroo say when she found that her baby was missing?
"Oh dear, my pocket's been picked!"

What would you get if you crossed a kangaroo with an airliner?
A jet that makes short hops.

Why did the kangaroo go to see a psychiatrist?
He wasn't feeling very jumpy.

What is the difference between a kangaroo and a lumberjack?
One hops and chews and the other chops and hews.

keepers

What did the keeper see when the elephant squirted water from his trunk?
A jumbo jet.

What do you call a motel keeper who peeks in the windows at night?
A sleeper-peeper keeper.

keeping

What can you keep when you give it away?
A cold.

What's the best way to keep fresh cookies?
Don't return them.

keys

What kind of a key can you eat?
A turkey.

In what key was "Home On the Range" originally written?
Beef flat.

What is the key to good breeding?
B natural.

killing

What is the surest way to make a killing on the stock market?
Buy sheep, sell deer.

Would you rather an elephant killed you, or a gorilla?
I'd rather he killed the gorilla.

kings

When is a piece of wood like a king?
When it is a ruler.

What was King Alfred called after he had burned the cake?
Alfred the Grate.

Who was the greatest king never crowned?
King Kong.

Why should a thoughtful king never be a fat one?
Because he is always a-thinking.

What is the difference between a king's son, a monkey's mother, a bald head, and an orphan?
A king's son is the heir apparent; a monkey's mother is a hairy parent; a bald head has no hair apparent; and an orphan has nary a parent.

Name the two kings that reign in America.
Smoking and soaking.

kisses
What is a kiss?
Nothing, divided by two.

Where in the Bible do we find the authority for women to kiss men?
"Whatsoever ye would that men should do unto you, do ye even so unto them."

Why is a kiss like gossip?
Because it goes from mouth to mouth.

How can you tell how a kiss is going to feel from its shape?
Because it is elliptical.

Why is a kiss from a pretty girl like a puppy dog in a refrigerator?
It is dog on ice.

kites
What kind of paper is best for kites?
Flypaper.

kittens
What is a kitten after it is four days old?
Five days old.

What did the kitten say to the tiger?
"Peace, brother!"

Why is a kitten biting her own tail like a good manager?
Because she makes both ends meet.

What is a knight's favorite fish?
A swordfish.

knees
Why do elephants have wrinkled knees?
From playing marbles.

If a boy should lose his knee, where can he get another?
At the butcher shop. That's where kidneys are sold.

knights
What is the most dangerous time for knights?
Nightfall.

How did the fallen knight explain his loss in the tournament?
"It was joust one of those things."

knives

A sharp knife cannot cut it,
Scissors cannot part it.
Water.

knots

Why do ships use knots instead of miles?
To keep the ocean tide.

Ku Klux Klan

How does the Ku Klux Klan come together?
They meet as estrangers in the night.

Q. Who can raise things without **lifting** them?

A. A farmer.

L

Why is L like your girl friend's trip to the beauty parlor?
Because it makes over a lover.

ladders

How can you fall off a fifty-foot ladder and not get hurt?
Fall off the bottom rung.

ladies

A lady in a boat with a yellow petticoat.
The moon.

What is the difference between a young lady and a man's hat?
One has feeling, and the other is felt.

lakes

What two things can fall on a lake and never even ripple the water?
Sunlight and moonbeams.

What North American lake is very frightening?
Lake Erie.

lameness

Why is a lame dog like a youngster adding six and seven?
Because he puts down three and carries one.

lamppost

What does the lamppost become when the lamp is removed?
A lamplighter.

Lancelot, Sir
Where did Sir Lancelot study?
In knight school.

land
How can you tell the land from the ocean?
One is dirty and the other is tidy.

language
What language should a language student study last?
The Finnish.

Lassie
Why was Lassie a famous dog in the movies?
Because she was always given the lead.

lateness
What is the difference between a person late for a train and a teacher at a school for girls?
One misses the train and the other trains the misses.

laughing
What should you do if you split your sides laughing?
Run until you get a stitch in them.

laundryman
What happened when Mrs. Harris backed into her laundryman?
He went down with flying collars.

laws
Why are laws like the ocean?
The most trouble is caused by the breakers.

lawyers
Why are lawyers like crows?
Because they like to have their cause heard.

Why would a pelican make a good lawyer?
He knows how to stretch his bill.

Why is it hard to get the best of a lawyer?
He always has his writs about him.

What is a lawyer's favorite pudding?
Suet.

Why are trial lawyers like the blades of gardening shears?
Because they don't cut each other—only what comes between them.

laxatives
Why should laxatives be taken in wafer form?
You just swallow one and wafer results.

laziness
Why did the lazy man try to get a job with a baker?
Because he thought it would be just the place for a good loaf.

Leaning Tower of Pisa, the
What makes the Leaning Tower of Pisa lean?
It never gets anything to eat.

left
Which is the left side of a pie?
The side that is left over.

legs
The riddle of the Sphinx: What goes on four legs in the morning, on two legs at noon, and on three in the evening?
(Think hard! The Sphinx killed everyone who couldn't solve this! When Oedipus finally did, the Sphinx turned to stone and has been sitting sulking in the Egyptian desert ever since.)

The answer?
Man. As a baby, he crawls on all fours. In the noon of life, he walks upright. In the evening of his time he uses a cane.

Here are some modern variations:

What has four legs and only one foot?
A bed.

What has legs but cannot walk?
A chair or a bed or a table.

Which animal has wooden legs?
A timber wolf.

What has no legs but *always* walks?
A shoe.

How many legs has a mule if you call a tail a leg?
Four. As Abraham Lincoln pointed out, if you call a tail a leg it is still a tail.

What is born first and gets its legs later?
The frog.

Two legs sat upon three legs;
One leg knocked two legs off three legs;

Two legs hit four legs with three legs.
A man sat on a three-legged stool milking a cow. The cow kicked him, and he hit her with the stool.

Long-legged (litheness)
Came to the door staffless,
More afraid of cock or hen
Than he was of dog or men.
A grasshopper.

What has eight legs, two arms, three heads, and wings?
The answer used to be: "A man on horseback with a hawk on his wrist." Today: "I don't know. Why don't you let me call Alcoholics Anonymous for you?"

lemons

What do you get when you feed lemons to a cat?
A sour puss.

How do you make a lemon drop?
Just let it fall.

length

What is it that gets longer and longer the more you cut off at each end?
A ditch.

When is a dog longer?
When he is let out.

What is the proper length to wear a dress?
Above two feet.

leopards

Why can't you trust the Indian leopard?
It's a cheetah.

Why is it hard for a leopard to hide?
Because it is always spotted.

What did the leopard say when it started to rain?
"That hits the spots!"

letters

What letter comes straight from the horse's mouth?
The first letter—it's an "A."

What three letters turn a girl into a woman?
A G E.

Why does *B* come before *C?*
Because a man must be before he can see.

What are the three most forceful letters in our alphabet?
N R G.

Which two contain nothing?
M T.

Can you name four letters that are used to address an ambassador?
X L N C.

Which are the four fattest letters we have, when you lump them together?
O B C T.

If you have to, what word of ten letters can you spell with five?
X P D N C.

Two letters often tempt mankind,
And those who yield will surely find
Two others ready to enforce
The punishment that comes of course.
X S and D K.

From a word of five letters take two and leave one.
Alone.

What letter is never in the alphabet?
The letter in the Post Office.

Why is opening a letter like a strange way of entering a room?
Because it means that you must break through the sealing.

What is it that if you take away all the letters will remain the same?
A postperson.

lettuce
Why is lettuce the most loving vegetable?
Because it is all heart.

liars
Why did the liar keep his word?
No one would take it.

libraries
Why did the firemen find putting out the fire at the library so dull?
They had to spend too long pouring over old books.

Why is the library not adding any more fairy tales?
They have run out of elf space.

Why are public libraries closed in wartime?
For fear that the magazines will blow up.

lice
What happened when the two lice moved to a new address?
They decided to give their friends a louse-warming party.

life
Why is life like this riddle?
Because you must give it up.

lifting
Who can raise things without lifting them?
A farmer.

lightness
What is very light but can't be lifted by the strongest person alive?
A bubble.

lightning
What do lightning and a weak person have in common?
Both have a shocking tendency to follow the line of least resistance.

lights
What kind of lights did Noah have on his Ark?
Flood lights.

Where was Moses when the lights went out?
In the dark.

What should you tell the electricity people if your house lights keep flashing on and off?
"A.C. come, A.C. go."

What are a thousand lights in a dish?
The stars.

limestone
What did the limestone say to the rock collector?
"Don't take me for granite."

Lincoln, Abraham
Why did President Lincoln's mail sometimes fail to reach him?
People sent it to his Gettysburg address.

Where was Lincoln going when he was thirty-nine years old?
Into his fortieth year.

lines

What puts the white lines on the ocean?
Ocean liners.

If a straight line is the shortest distance between two points, what is a bee line?
The shortest distance between two buzz stops.

lineups

What is the difference between the end of a long lineup and a letter box?
One makes the tail and the other takes the mail.

lions

How many lions can you put in an empty cage?
One. After that the cage is not empty.

What is the best way to talk to a roaring lion?
By long distance.

Why is a lion in the desert like Christmas?
Because of its sandy claws.

liquids

What liquid can't freeze?
Boiling water.

liquor

Why is a preference for corn liquor like a well-marked road?
Because you can't go awry.

little

When will Little always chase out Big?
When a little lamp chases out the darkness.

Too little for one,
Not right for two,
Too much for three.
Anger.

Little Bo Peep

How did Little Bo Peep lose her sheep?
She had a crook with her.

Why did she really dread their return?
Because she knew from the poem that she would find their tales a drag.

lives

What has more lives than a cat?
A frog. It croaks every night.

loans

What kind of person makes a good loans officer for a bank?
Someone who takes a lot of interest in his work.

London

What part of London is in France?
The letter N.

Long Island

How do sailors recognize Long Island?
By the Sound.

lookers

Two lookers,
Two crookers,
Four standers,
One switch-about.
A cow.

looking

Why is it that whenever you are looking for anything, you always find it in the
last place you look?
Because you always stop looking when you find it.

loss

A man buys a pair of shoes for $30 and hands the shoe clerk a $100 bill. The
clerk goes into the grocery store to have it changed; he comes back and gives
the man $70. When the man has gone, the grocer comes in and says, "That
was a counterfeit bill you gave me!" The shoe clerk gives him a good bill. How
much has the shoe store lost?
Seventy dollars and the shoes.

loudness

Why do chess players wear loud socks?
To keep their feet from falling asleep.

Lourdes

Why are the people who visit the famous shrine at Lourdes like the American
people after a presidential election?
They expect miracles.

How do you get to Lourdes?
Icon down the road a piece.

love

How can you measure the depth of a man's love?
By his sighs.

As you get older, how does love strike you?
It often seems jejune in January.

What does man love more than life,
Hate more than death or mortal strife;
That which contented men desire,
The poor have, the rich require;
The miser spends, the spendthrift saves,
And all men carry to their graves?
Nothing.

lovers

What is the difference between her rejected husband and her secret lover?
One misses the kisses and the other kisses the Mrs.

luck

When is it bad luck to have a cat follow you?
When you are a mouse.

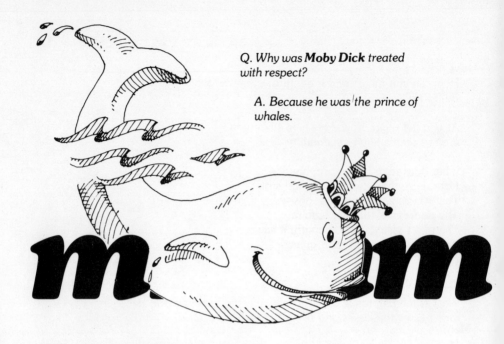

Q. Why was **Moby Dick** treated with respect?

A. Because he was the prince of whales.

M

Why is the letter M so important to you?
Because without it your mother would be some other.

Why should you never put the letter M into the refrigerator?
Because it will change ice into mice.

made

Formed long ago, yet made today,
Employed while others sleep,
What few would like to give away,
Nor any wish to keep.
A bed.

madmen

Why is a madman like two ordinary men?
Because he is beside himself.

magazines

What magazine would be likely to give the best report of a fire?
A powder magazine.

magnets

What did the little magnet say to the big magnet?
"I find you very attractive."

mail

Why did the girl give up the mail carrier for the grocery clerk?
She was tired of waiting for the past man's ring.

Where do monsters get their mail?
At the dead-letter office.

making

What can you make that you can't see?
Noise.

The man that made it sold it.
The man that bought it didn't want it.
The man that used it didn't know it.
What was it?
A coffin.

What is it that was made years ago and I just made again today?
My bed.

What is the best thing to make in a hurry?
Haste.

Malone, Molly

What could you tell about Molly Malone as she wheeled her wheelbarrow
through streets broad and narrow?
She was a shellfish girl.

marble

In marble walls as white as milk,
Lined with skin as soft as silk,
Within a fountain crystal clear,
A golden apple doth appear.
No doors there are to this stronghold,
Yet thieves break in and steal the gold.
An egg.

mares

The Irish ask:
A white mare in the lake and she does not wet her foot?
The moon.

margarine

Why did the city girl name her first daughter Margarine?
Because she didn't have any but her.

marksmen

What is the difference between a good marksman and a violin case?
One finds the middle and the other minds the fiddle.

marriage

What should you do if your marriage is on the rocks?
Try buying a bed.

Why is marriage so often like a wagon train surrounded by Indians?
Because those who are in it wish to be out and those who are out wish to be in.

Who marries many women but stays single all his life?
A priest.

Why did the young lady who was out for a walk sit down and cry when she heard that her mother was remarrying?
She could not go a step father.

marshmallows
Why did the elephant sit on the marshmallow?
To keep from falling into the hot chocolate.

Martians
What were the first words spoken by a Martian on landing here?
"We didn't planet this way."

What happened to Ray when he was eaten by a Martian?
He became X-Ray.

martini
What do you call a martini served without an olive or twist?
The Dickens.

masochists
Why did the masochist tie a lion, a tiger, and a crocodile to the foot of her bed?
She liked to have a few bites before going to sleep.

massage
Why do people go to massage parlors?
Everyone likes to feel a little kneaded.

matches
Why was the inventor of the safety match so pleased?
Because it was a striking success.

May
If April showers bring May flowers, what do May flowers bring?
Pilgrims.

If you saw a jar with the label "May Bee" on it, what could you suspect it contained?
Synthetic honey.

mayonnaise
What did the mayonnaise say to the refrigerator?
"Please shut the door. I'm dressing!"

Mecca

How would you describe the social set in Mecca?
The chic of Araby.

medical officers

Why did the alcoholic medical officer get transferred to an artillery unit?
He already had a caisson.

medicine

When is medicine first mentioned in the Bible?
When God gave Moses two tablets.

Why did Chuck tiptoe past the medicine chest?
He didn't want to wake the sleeping pills.

medicine men

What's the best way for a medicine man to keep fit?
He must exorcise.

men

Who invented the first mechanical man?
Frank N. Stein.

Suppose there were only one tree left in the world, and one man, and one ax! The man cuts down the tree with the ax but the one tree falls and kills the one man. Who is left to tell the tale?
The women.

What kind of men are very apt to worship their maker?
Self-made ones.

How many big men have been born in Alaska?
None. Only babies.

What is it that a man never can have and yet can give to a woman?
A husband.

mermaids

What does a mermaid use to tie up her hair?
A marine band.

mice

When are mice and rats unhappy?
When it's raining cats and dogs.

Why is a mouse that is moving like an elephant?
They both have to take their trunks along.

What is the difference between a mouse and a miss?
One harms the cheese and the other charms the he's.

Why is a mouse like hay?
The cat'll eat it.

microphones
Is it true that an Irishman invented the microphone?
No. It is purely a patent mike story.

Midas
Why did Midas the King hang his head?
He had a gilt complex.

Middle Ages, the
Why are the Middle Ages called the Dark Ages?
Because there were so many knights.

midgets
Why did the circus's lady midget hate the fat man?
Because she couldn't bear him.

What did the midget say when asked to lend money?
"Sorry! I'm a little short!"

milk
Name six things that have milk in them.
Butter, cheese, ice cream, a milkshake, and two cows.

What happened to the milking contest?
It ended in udder chaos.

How do you keep milk from turning sour?
Leave it in the cow.

What runs through the streets with one horn and gives milk?
A milk truck.

millionaires
Why must a millionaire be an intelligent fellow?
Because he has a lot of cents.

miners
Why is an underground coal miner like a beautician?
Because they are both face workers.

mines
I am taken from a mine and shut up in a wooden case from which I am never

released and yet I am used by nearly everybody.
A pencil.

minimum
What is a minimum?
A small mother.

ministers
The village minister and his wife, the school teacher and his daughter, were walking in the woods. They found a bird's nest that contained four eggs. Each of them took out an egg and yet left one in the nest.
There was only one woman; the minister had married the teacher's daughter.

minutes
What comes once in a minute, once in a month, but never in a hundred years?
The letter M.

Where is Minute Street?
Between Sixty-first and Sixty-third.

miracles
When does a farmer perform miracles?
When he turns his horse to grass and he turns his cow to pasture.

What is a common miracle in Ireland?
Waking the dead.

mirrors
What is the difference between some vain people and their mirrors?
The people talk without reflecting and the mirrors reflect without talking.

Why should you practice your jokes by telling them to your mirror?
If they're good, you may see it crack up.

mirth
By a change of punctuation, how can you turn mirth into crime?
By making man's laughter manslaughter.

missionaries
Why are missionaries popular with cannibals?
Because they go down very well with them.

Mississippi
If Mississippi should lend Missouri her New Jersey, what would Delaware?
She might have just her Yukon.

Missouri
What was President Truman's explanation for his home state's hospitality?
"Missouri loves company."

mittens

Why do shy girls wear mittens?
To keep off the chaps.

moats

Why should you never listen to people who have just come out of a moat?
Because they are all wet.

If you own a castle, why is it better to have two moats built instead of one?
That way, you will get the moats for your money.

Moby Dick

Why was Moby Dick treated with respect?
Because he was the prince of whales.

models

What makes modeling such a crazy business?
It can turn you into a mannequin a moment.

molecules

What is the first thing you should know about the molecule?
How to keep it from falling out of your eye when you sneeze.

money

What is so strange about money?
You have to make it first before you can make it last.

If all the money in the world were to be divided equally among all the people what would each one get?
An equal share.

What is the easiest way to make money?
Crumple it up. Right away, you'll find it in creases.

Where is making money frowned upon?
In a socialist state. There, a profit is without honor.

How can you make money fast?
Glue it down.

Why should you keep some money in your refrigerator?
So that you will always have some cold cash.

What is the hardest money to change or get rid of?
Matrimony.

Why do Texans feed their cows money?
So that they can get rich milk.

monkeys

Why are monkeys always chattering?
Each one has a tail.

What kind of monkey eats chips?
A chipmunk.

What is another name for a silly monkey?
A chumpanzee.

How do you get a one-armed monkey down from an orange tree?
Wave at him.

What sort of monkey has a sweet tooth?
A meringue-outang.

monocles

What happens when two monocles get together and make spectacles of themselves?
They create glass distinction.

monsters

What do you say when you meet a two-headed monster?
"Hello, hello!"

What do you do with a blue monster?
Cheer him up.

Why do monster families stay together for so long?
Because they can't stand to kiss each other good-bye.

How does a monster count to thirteen?
On its fingers.

What is a monster's normal eyesight?
20/20/20/20/20.

Why don't monsters make good dancers?
Because they have three left feet.

What do sea monsters eat?
Fish and ships.

What does a monster do when he loses a hand?
Goes to a second-hand store.

What do you get when you cross a monster with a drip-dry suit?
A wash-and-werewolf.

months

Which month has twenty-eight days in it?
All months do.

What are the warmest months of the year?
September, November, and December. They all have embers in them.

moons

What did the moon say to the star?
"Boy, are you far out!"

Which is heavier, a half moon or a full moon?
A half moon, because a full moon is lighter.

What is the moon worth?
A dollar, because it has four quarters.

Why can't the man in the moon afford to get married?
Because he only gets one quarter a week.

What is the reason no one would marry the man in the moon?
Because he is out all night.

moose

How do you define a moose?
A member of the deer family and its elk.

morons

Why did the moron push his bed into the fireplace?
Because he wanted to sleep like a log.

Why did the moron throw the clock out the window?
Because he wanted to see time fly.

Why did the moron stuff his father in the refrigerator?
He wanted cold pop.

Moses

Why did Moses have to be hidden quickly when he was a baby?
Saving him was a rush job.

Moslems

Why do Moslems prostrate themselves?
It's not the heat, it's the humility.

mosquitoes

What is the difference between someone who has just been bitten by a mosquito and a runner waiting to race?
One is going to itch and the other is itching to go.

motels
What passes many motels without moving?
The highway.

mothers-in-law
What is a man that eats his mother-in-law?
Gladiator.

Mother Superior
What was the Mother Superior's secret for her success?
Efface was her fortune.

moths
Why did the moth eat through the carpeting?
He wanted to see the floor show.

mountains
Why do so few people take up mountain climbing?
Because it gives you an eyrie feeling.

How did the big mountain know the little mountain was a liar?
Because it was only a bluff.

mourners
Why are professional mourners so noisy?
They are trying to eek out a living.

mousetraps
How do you spell mousetrap in three letters?
C A T.

mouths
What has a mouth but can't talk?
A river.

movies
What would you do if a hippopotamus sat in front of you at the movies?
Miss most of the movie.

Why is an astronomer like a tour guide on a movie lot?
They both make their living from star gazing.

moving
What is larger than you are, moves silently, and leaves no path?
A canoe.

mules
What is your reward when you tickle a mule?
You get a big kick out of it.

murmurs

I often murmur, but never weep;
Always in bed but never asleep.
My mouth, much larger than my head,
Though always open is never fed.
I have no feet, yet swiftly run.
Yet have to fall before I'm done.
A river.

music

You may get a charge out of this one from India:
Music drops from heaven. But who is the player?
Lightning (which makes thunder).

By the way, what is the first thing to do if you want to hear a little Indian music?
Find a baby sitar.

In music, what does "allegro" mean?
A line of chorus girls.

musicians

Why did the novice horn player get fired?
Because when he came to a tacit passage he blew it.

Musketeers, the Three

Why have the Three Musketeers had so much public appeal?
They were pretty fency fellows.

myths

What is a myth?
Thome-one who ithn't a mithith.

Why is it a myth to consider the owl wise?
Because there is no fool like an owl fool.

*Q. Why do some elephants wear red **nail polish**?*

A. So they can hide behind rose bushes. (These are known as bush elephants; not to be confused with bull elephants—they hide in the bullrushes.)

N

Why is the letter *N* like a pig?
Because it makes a sty nasty.

How can you make *N* jealous?
Adding V to it will create N V.

Why is *N* like summer?
Because it makes ice nice.

nail polish

Why do some elephants wear red nail polish?
So they can hide behind rose bushes. (These are known as bush elephants; not to be confused with bull elephants—they hide in the bullrushes.)

nails

When shouldn't you hit a nail with a hammer?
When it's on someone's toe.

Why is a nail fast in the wall like an old man?
Because it is in firm.

names

What girl's name, besides Anna, reads the same both ways?
Hannah.

What is this name you should not scorn?
There was a man who was not born,
His father was not before him.
He did not live, he did not die.
His epitaph is not o'er him.
A man by the name of Nott.

naming

Why did Uncle Oscar name both of his sons Ed?
Because he had heard that two Eds are better than one.

Name me and you destroy me.
Silence.

Naomi

In the Bible, what was Naomi's final comment on her girl friend?
"Ruth is stranger than fiction."

napkins

Who would eat at a king's table and without using a napkin?
A fly.

nations

What nation has always overcome in the end?
Determination.

What is the most warlike nation?
Vaccination, because it is almost always in arms.

Nature

What is the best time to study Nature's book?
When Autumn turns the leaves.

necks

What has a neck but no head?
A bottle.

What has a neck but no head, two arms but no hands?
A shirt.

It goes all over the hills and plains,
But when it comes to a river, it breaks its neck.
A path.

needles

What carries hundreds of needles but never sews?
A porcupine.

never
Tell me something that never was and never, never shall be.
A mouse's nest in a cat's ear.

newspapers
What did the cavemen call their newspaper?
The Prehistoric Times.

When is a newspaper story the sharpest?
When it is filed.

What is the proper newspaper for invalids?
The Weekly News.

Why should "Watermelon" be a good name for a newspaper?
Because its insides would really be read!

Newton, Isaac
Legend has it that Isaac Newton discovered gravity when an apple hit him on the head. What was the result?
The discovery shook him to the core.

Niagara Falls
What is the difference between Niagara Falls and Queen Elizabeth the First?
One is a wonder and the other was a Tudor.

nickels
What is the difference between an old nickel and a new penny?
Four cents.

night caps
What is the difference between a young girl and a nightcap?
One is born to wed and the other is worn to bed.

nihilism
Can you explain nihilism?
It's how the Egyptians pyramided their profits.

Noah
What did Noah say just as he got the boat finished?
"Ark, I think it's raining!"

noise
What makes more noise under a gate than a stuck pig?
Two stuck pigs.

noses
Why is your nose in the middle of your face?
Because it is the scenter.

Why isn't a dog's nose twelve inches long?
Because if it were it would be a foot.

What is it that has nothing left but a nose when it loses an eye?
The word noise.

Why is the nose on your face like the V in "civility?"
Because it's between two eyes.

What's wrong with you if your nose runs and your feet smell?
You're built upside down.

Why are your nose and your handkerchief like deadly enemies?
Because they seldom meet without coming to blows.

nothing

What is it that is too much for one, enough for two, but nothing at all for three?
A secret.

There is a thing that nothing is,
And yet it has a name;
'Tis sometimes tall and sometimes short,
It joins our walk, it joins our sport,
And plays at every game.
Your shadow.

nudists

Why do nudists have plenty of time to spare?
Because they have nothing on.

What did the Jewish boy do when he came of age in the nudist colony?
He had a bare Mitzvah.

nudity

Why do you have to be careful about painting people in the nude?
You could catch cold.

numbers

Why should the number 288 never be mentioned in polite company?
Because it is two gross.

nurseries

What is a nursery?
A bawl room.

If your rich uncle sent you $10 toward setting up a nursery for your new baby,
what would you call his gift?
A cursory nursery bursary.

nurses

How do pretty nurses handle the advances of young doctors in training?
They take them all intern.

Why do women from India usually make good nurses?
Because they know how to care for the Sikh.

nutcrackers

What sort of animals use nutcrackers?
Toothless squirrels.

nuts

What kind of nut has some of its inside outside?
A doughnut.

Why are crazy people called nuts?
Because when you come to deal with them they are cracked.

Q. Mr. Twiddle bet Mr. Twaddle that he could eat more **oysters**. Mr. Twiddle ate ninety and Mr. Twaddle ate a hundred and one. How many more did Mr. Twaddle eat than Mr. Twiddle?

A. Ten. As we said, he ate a hundred and won.

O

In what common word does the vowel O sound like the letter I?
In "women."

Why is the vowel O the only one sounded?
Because all the others are in audible.

oaks

What is the difference between an oak tree and a tight shoe?
One makes acorns and the other makes corns ache.

If oaks come from acorns, where do oars come from?
Oarhouses.

What is the safest way to get to the top of an oak tree?
Sit on an acorn and wait for it to grow.

oats

How do you know that horses really don't like oats?
They always say neigh to them.

oboes

What is the difference between an oboe and a flute?
An oboe is an American transient and a flute is an Oriental homosexual.

oceans

How do you know that an ocean is friendly?
Because it waves.

Then why does the ocean roar?
Because it has crabs in its bed.

What lies at the bottom of the ocean and shakes?
A nervous wreck.

Why do our laws resemble oceans?
Because most of our trouble is caused by the breakers.

octopuses
What did the boy octopus say to the girl octopus?
"I want to hold your hand, hand, hand, hand, hand, hand, hand, hand."

oddity
What is the oddest city there is?
Eccentricity.

Which is the odd fellow, the one who asks a question or the one who answers?
The one who asks, because he is the querist.

When the first part of a certain odd number is removed it becomes even. What number is it?
Seven.

officers
If a girl visiting an army camp will only go out with the officers, what can you conclude about her?
That she is rotten to the corps.

Why are girls so fond of officers?
Because every girl likes a good offer, sir.

offices
Why is it absurd to call a dentist's office a dental parlor?
Because it is the drawing room.

oil
What is oil before it is pumped out of the ground?
A well-kept secret.

Oklahoma
What do they call lumberjacks in Oklahoma?
Oakies.

oldness
What is the best way of defining an old maid?
One who will only go so far and no fervor.

What is the best advice you can offer to incipient old maids?
Better elate than never.

Why does a badly sung song resemble an old man's head?
Because it is often terribly bawled.

An old woman in a red coat was crossing a field in which there was a goat.
What strange transformation came over her?
When she saw the goat turn to butter, she became a scarlet runner.

What is the name of the oldest whistler in the world—and what is the name of
the first tune whistled?
The wind, whistling "Over the Hills and Far Away."

Oliver Twist
Why did Oliver Twist get into trouble?
Someone was urchin him on.

one
Why is one the most important number?
It is the only number by which all other numbers can be divided.

What two letters spell a number less than 100?
A T

onions
What happens when you peel onions?
You get a leeky eye.

Why does an onion resemble a ringing bell?
Because in an onion it's just one peel after another.

openings
Why is an off-Broadway opening like fertilizer?
Because it's usually awful.

Where should you go first to look for a job with plenty of good openings?
Apply to be a hotel doorman.

opera
Why is the interior of an old opera house a sorry sight?
Because the boxes are in tiers.

Why does a Good Humor man resemble an opera singer?
Because he gives out ice creams.

operators
What is the surest way to become a big time operator?
Get a job winding clocks in steeples.

operations
What is the greatest surgical operation ever performed?
Lansing, Michigan.

opposites
What word, by changing the position of one letter, becomes its opposite?
United—untied.

opticians
How would you describe an optician's office?
A site for sore eyes.

What is the difference between an optician and an optimist?
An optician checks the eyes and an optimist checks the sighs.

orange
What did the little chick say when it found an orange in its nest?
"Look at the orange Mama laid!"

orders
If unsolicited orders come in "over the transom," how do rumors of possible orders arrive?
Innuendo.

Orient, the
What tree would be worn in the Orient?
The sandalwood.

ornithologists
What is the difference between an ornithologist and a bad speller?
One is a bird watcher and the other is a word botcher.

Oscars
If a cat won an Oscar, what would she get?
An Acatemy Award.

outfielders
What insect would make the best outfielder?
A spider. It's great at catching flies.

out
If you are locked out what should you do?
Sing songs until you find one with the right key.

outhouses
How do you get an elephant into an outhouse?
Open the door.

What do you call outhouse inspectors?
The Privy Council.

overeating
Why should you avoid overeating?
It makes you thick to your stomach.

overlooking
What is it that everyone, no matter how careful, overlooks?
A nose.

owls
Why was the father owl worried about the baby owl?
Because he didn't give a hoot about anything.

What was the father owl's first advice to his son?
"It's not 'What?' you know, it's 'Whooo?' you know."

oxen
In Nigeria, they puzzle over things like this:
A thousand oxen are going along and do not raise a dust.
Ants.

Oxford
What are the basic requirements for admission to Oxford University?
You must be both a gentleman and a sculler.

oxygen
If you breathe oxygen in the daytime, what do you breathe in the nighttime?
Nitrogen.

oysters
Why should you eat oysters?
For mussel tone.

When are oysters like fretful people?
When they are in a stew.

Why is an oyster like a man of sense?
Because he knows how to keep his mouth shut.

Mr. Twiddle bet Mr. Twaddle that he could eat more oysters. Mr. Twiddle ate ninety and Mr. Twaddle ate a hundred and one. How many more did Mr. Twaddle eat than Mr. Twiddle?
Ten. As we said, he ate a hundred and won.

*Q. What did the head **priest** say when the young priest asked if he could date a nun?*

A. "Yes, my son. But don't get into the habit."

P

Why is a selfish person like the letter *P*?
Because he is the first in pity and the last in help.

Why should a stupid student study the letter *P* before taking a test?
Because it can make an ass pass.

pachyderms

What is a cheerful pachyderm?
A happy-potamus.

pain

What pain do we make light of?
Window pane.

painters

What did the painter say to the wall?
"One more crack and I'll plaster you!"

painting

What's the best way to paint a rabbit?
With hare spray.

pajamas

Why are pajamas like prostitutes?
They are both worn in bed.

paleness
> Why was the patient a little pale?
> *He had almost kicked the bucket.*

pants
> Why did the drunk put his pants on backward?
> *Because he didn't know whether he was coming or going.*

> What should you do when you wear your pants out?
> *Wear them in again.*

paper
> What kind of paper can you tear?
> *Terrible paper.*

> What kind of paper is most like a sneeze?
> *Tissue.*

parents
> What is the difference between your parents and a tongue-tied lunatic?
> *One is mum and dad and the other is dumb and mad.*

parking
> What could happen if you parked a yellowish-brown car in the desert?
> *When you came back you might not be able to find the khaki.*

parrots
> Why was the parrot alarmed when he flew into the taxidermist's shop by mistake?
> *He noted it was a stuffy place and watched what was going on with mounting apprehension.*

> What do you get when you cross a parrot with an elephant?
> *An animal that tells what it remembers.*

parting
> What is the easiest thing in the world to part with?
> *A comb.*

parts
> What is never part of anything?
> *The whole.*

patients
> What did the patient say to the anesthetist?
> *"Because of you, I've been considerably put out!"*

Patrick, Saint

It can't be true that Saint Patrick drove *all* the snakes out of Ireland; you still hear the Irish talk and sing about one to this day. What is it called?
The Emerald Eel.

patriotism

Why is a railroad exceedingly patriotic?
It is bound to the country with strong ties.

Pavlov

Explain why Pavlov's experiments with a dog were so important.
They became the salivation of psychology.

peaches

How do you make a peach cordial?
Buy her a few drinks.

peacocks

If my peacock lays an egg in your yard, who owns the egg?
Peahens lay eggs.

Why does the peacock fan his feathers?
To let the peahens see him putting on a spread.

Why is a 9 like a peacock?
Because it's nothing without a tail.

peanut butter

What do you get when you cross peanut butter with an elephant?
Either peanut butter with a long memory or an elephant that sticks to the roof of your mouth.

peanuts

What is the difference between peanuts and cashews?
Those who work for peanuts are always shelling out. It's those with cashew can salt some away.

Peary, Admiral

What did Admiral Peary's wife say on the eve of his departure for the South Pole?
"Peritonitis the night!"

peas

Why is it dangerous for farmers to plant peas during a war?
The enemy might come along and shell them.

How many peas in a pint?
One.

peasants

What is the difference between the Russian peasant and the czar?
The peasant was penniless and the czar was Nicholas.

peeking

What goes round and round the house and peeks in every window?
The sun.

Peeping Tom

What is the difference between a Peeping Tom and someone just out of the bathtub?
One is rude and nosy and the other is nude and rosy.

What four letters should frighten away a Peeping Tom?
O I C U!

What do you call a female Peeping Tom?
A Virginia Peeper.

pelicans

Why couldn't the pelican charge any more groceries?
Because he had too large a bill.

pencils

Why is a pencil like a riddle?
It's no good without a point.

What is the biggest pencil in the world?
Pennsylvania.

What is the difference between a horse and a pencil?
You can drive a horse to water but a pencil must be lead.

What did one pencil say to the other?
"I've got a leadache."

Why is a lead pencil like a perverse child?
Because it never does write by itself.

Why should you do your arithmetic lessons with a pencil?
Because the pencil can't do them without you.

pennies

What did the penny say to the dime?
"It would make more cents if we went together."

What happened when the young cat swallowed a penny?
There was money in the kitty.

pens
Who invented the first pen?
The Incas.

What kind of a pen does a plagiarist use?
Steel.

What pen should never be used in writing?
A sheep pen.

people
What kinds of people should you have around you when you are very tired?
Nodding acquaintances.

percussion
Why do you have to have special training for the percussion section of an orchestra?
Banging together brass plates is not as cymbal as it looks.

perfume
Why is perfume never moved without orders?
Because it is scent wherever it goes.

personality
Which artist had an arresting personality?
Constable.

How do psychiatrists treat a dual personality?
They usually ask one of them to wait outside.

Peter, Saint
When you finally approach the Pearly Gates, how will Saint Peter greet you?
"Well, halo there!"

pharmacists
What is a pharmacist?
A pharm hand.

philosophers
What do a philosopher and an airplane pilot have in common?
Both believe that to air is human.

photographers
At what age is it best to start out to be a press photographer?
In the flash of youth.

physics
What is the advantage of having nuclear physics?
It is better than the old, clouded kind.

pianists
> What can you assume if a pianist has a light touch?
> *That he has a flare for the piano.*

pianos
> Why is a piano like an eye?
> *Because they are both closed when their lids are down.*

> When is a fish like a piano?
> *When you tuna fish.*

pictures
> What did the picture say to the wall?
> *"First they frame me, then they hang me!"*

> Why would anyone hang that picture?
> *Because they couldn't find the artist!*

pies
> What is the best thing to put into pies?
> *Your teeth.*

> What will make pies sneaky?
> *The letter S makes spies of them.*

pigeons
> Why did the pigeon fly over the racetrack?
> *Because he wanted to have a flutter on the horses.*

pigs
> Why is a pig one of the most wonderful animals in the farmyard?
> *Because it is killed before it is cured.*

> Why do little pigs eat so much?
> *Because they want to make hogs of themselves.*

> When is it proper to refer to a person as a pig?
> *When he is a boar.*

> Why did the farmer name the pig "Ink"?
> *Because it kept running out of the pen.*

> What do you call someone who steals pigs?
> *A hamburgler.*

pigsties
> Why do Canadian farmers build their pigsties directly between the house and the barn?
> *For the pigs.*

Pilgrims, the

What were the first two things that the Pilgrims did when they landed in America?
First they fell on their knees, then they fell on the aborigines.

What did the Indians say when they saw the Pilgrims coming ashore?
"Well, there goes the neighborhood!"

pilots

What did the grounded pilot say when he saw the weather report?
"If the fog lifts it won't be mist."

Why does a glider pilot dislike to talk about his flights?
It is generally a soar point with him.

pines

Why did the pine tree pine?
Because it saw a weeping willow.

What kind of pine has the sharpest needles?
A porcupine.

pins

Why is a careful man like a pin?
Because his head prevents him from going too far.

Why is a bad pin like a broken pencil?
Because it has no point.

pirates

Why does a pirate need a great deal of sand?
Because he scours the seas.

Why did the pirates have to give up hauling their prisoners under their ships?
They were keeling too many people.

pitchers

Why do little pitchers have big ears?
From listening to the coach.

What is the difference between a pitcher of water and a man throwing his wife over a bridge?
One is water in the pitcher and the other is pitch her in the water.

planes

If a plane crashed on the U.S.–Canadian border, in which country would you bury the survivors?
They don't bury survivors.

planets

What did the little planet say when it broke out of orbit?
"Look Mom, no gravities!"

plants

When is a plant like a hog?
When it begins to root.

What plant is fatal to mice?
Catnip.

plates

Sometimes it is a plate,
Sometimes it is a long, thin boat.
What is it?
The moon.

plays

What do you call the person who sees to it that a play runs smoothly?
A stagedriver.

Why was *East Lynne* such a famous play in its time?
It was a mellow drama.

pleasant

How would you define "pleasant"?
A Japanese farmer.

plowing

What is often plowed, but never planted?
Snow.

Why is a plowed field like feathered game?
Because it's part ridges.

pockets

Why is an empty pocket always the same?
Because there is no change in it. On the other hand . . .

How can your pocket be empty and still have something in it?
It can have a hole in it.

poetry

What is the best way to describe poetry that lacks punctuation?
Breathless prose.

poets

Why is a poet about to approach an editor like an aging actress?
Because both are facing a decline.

polecats
Why is a polecat a very aristocratic animal?
Because it is a member of high society.

policemen
How do you know that policemen are strong?
Because they can hold up traffic with just one hand.

Why is a policeman's job very tricky?
Because there are a lot of catches in his work.

What happens when a policeman takes a burglar's fingerprints?
It creates a very bad impression.

What was the artistic policeman's favorite subject?
Drawing his gun.

What did the policeman say after booking a dozen motorists for illegal parking?
"I've done a fine day's work."

politeness
What is the difference between a loaf of good pumpernickel and a polite young lady?
One is well-made bread and the other is a well-bred maid.

politicians
Why is fraternity among politicians relatively rare?
There is too much quibbling rivalry.

In what month do politicians talk the least?
February. It's the shortest month.

Why is a politician like someone who lines up for the movies?
Because he stands in order to get a seat.

When Chinese politicians get into a heated debate, what is it called?
A tongue war.

Why did the dishonest politician flee the country?
He decided that a change was as good as arrest.

pollution
What did the polluted water say to the filter?
"I hope I make myself clear."

ponies
What do you call a pony with a sore throat?
A little hoarse.

What kinds of girls wear ponytails?
Those that like to horse around.

popularity
Why are Norwegians so popular at parties?
They have a troll sense of humor.

porcupines
What did the baby porcupine say to the cactus?
"Is that you, Mamma?"

What do you get when you cross a porcupine with a goat?
A kid that's hard to handle.

Porky Pig
How does Porky Pig explain his success as an actor?
"I ham what I ham!"

Porter, Cole
What did his biographer say to Cole Porter?
"Let's beguine at the beginning."

portraits
Why are painted portraits like tins of sardines?
Because they are usually done in oils.

postmaster
If the postmaster went to a circus and a bear ate him, what time would it be?
8 p.m.

postmen
Why are postmen very learned people?
Because they are men of letters.

post offices
Why should women be employed in the post office?
Because they can manage the males.

posts
If a cat can't find a post on which to sharpen its claws, what else could it use?
How about a caterpillar?

potatoes
Where were potatoes first found?
In the ground.

Why should potatoes grow better than other vegetables?
Because they have eyes to see what they are doing.

What is the difference between a potato and a soldier?
One shoots from the eye and the other from the shoulder.

When did the Irish potato change nationality?
When it became French fried.

What is the difference between a diseased potato and a beehive?
Not any—one is a specked tater and the other is a bee holder.

When are potatoes used for mending clothes?
When they are put in patches.

pots
How does a coffeepot feel when it's full?
Perky.

Why did the pot call the kettle black?
Because that got the kettle all steamed up.

power
Name one consequence of the decline of British power in India.
The English residents went through a great deal of gin and jitters.

power play
What should you do if you want your team to make a power play?
Erg them on.

preserves
What did the worker in the preserves factory say after his first week on the job?
"It's just one jam thing after another!"

presidents
You and the president both did the same thing yesterday. What was it?
Breathe.

Why is the job of president like a back tooth?
Because it is hard to fill well.

prices
Why should you never complain about the price of an airplane ticket?
They only charge what's fare.

priests
Why did the virile young man leave the priesthood?
He found the mission impossible.

What did the head priest say when the young priest asked if he could date a nun?
"Yes, my son. But don't get into the habit."

Why does a priest sound different once he's in the pulpit?
That's not the priest up there—that's his altar ego.

How do priests get back at their mothers?
They have a Stabat Mater.

prisoners

What did the prisoners say when the jail was flooded?
"Would someone please bail us out?"

producers

When is a movie producer like an astronomer?
When he discovers a new star.

professors

What did the college professor scrawl on the essay?
"Thesis awful!"

How do you explain to an English professor that you're not interested in becoming the second Shakespeare?
"I contrite a thing."

pronunciation

What word is pronounced quicker by adding a syllable to it?
Quick.

prostitutes

What would you call a group of mining-town prostitutes?
A smelting of ores.

What is the difference between a prostitute and a soldier?
One powders the face and the other faces the powder.

What is the difference between a prostitute and a high-wire artist?
One is a street walker and the other is a straight walker.

Name the early Shakespearean play about the price of prostitutes.
Love's Labour's Cost.

What is the difference between an aging prostitute and a burglar?
One wears false locks and the other false keys.

proverbs

What proverb must a lawyer avoid?
He must not take the will for the deed.

puddings

What is the difference between someone who enjoys rice pudding and a

greedy storekeeper?
One's a rice praiser and the other is a price raiser.

Why is a plum pudding like the ocean?
Because it contains many currants.

Puerto Rico
What is black and white and lives in Puerto Rico?
A lost penguin.

punning
What is meant by punning?
Punishment.

Why are so few books written about punning?
An inveterate punster is not a chapter give in.

puns
At what time is a pun most effective?
When it strikes you.

Why is a bad pun like a greenhorn on a bucking bronco?
It doesn't sit well.

Why is a good pun like a good cat?
Because it requires pause.

What is the soundest observation you can make about the pun in the title of
the play *The Importance of Being Earnest?*
It was a Wilde idea.

puppies
If a puppy loses its tail, where can it go for another?
To a retail store.

Why is an untrained puppy like a twenty-five-cent piece?
It has a head, a tail, and two sides—and it's a bit rough around the edges.

purple
What is purple and 5,000 miles long?
The Grape Wall of China.

pushing
What could a little man push in a wheelbarrow that a big man could not?
The big man.

putt
What's red and goes putt putt putt?
A sunburned golf addict.

pyramids

How would you define an Egyptian pyramid?
A tomb with a view.

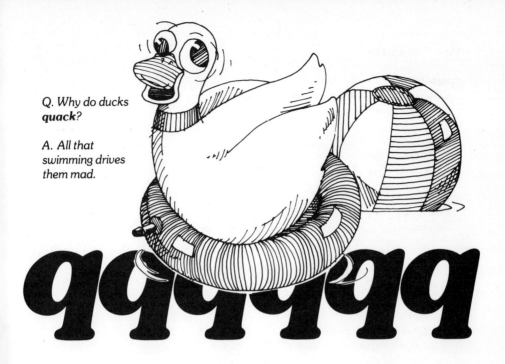

Q. Why do ducks quack?

A. All that swimming drives them mad.

Q

Why is Q the letter least likely to get lost?
Because actors and musicians all watch for it.

quacks

Why are phony doctors called quacks?
Because when the police show up they duck.

Why do ducks quack?
All that swimming drives them mad.

quadrangle

What is a quadrangle?
An argument outside a private school or college.

quakes

Why is it bad to try and make a soufflé during a quake?
Because you can't have your quake and eat it.

qualms

What kind of qualm do you have most frequently?
The qualm before the storm.

quarrels

What flower is like a girl who has had a quarrel with her boyfriend?
The bluebell.

What is a quarrelsome city called?
Pugnacity.

quarters
Why are soldiers often confined to quarters?
To keep them from getting rich through gambling.

quash
What does "quash" mean?
It's a game played by judges in quash courts.

quasi
Give a sentence demonstrating the proper use of "quasi."
All actors are quasi—and some sailors are quasi in the head.

queens
Who comes into the queen's bedchamber without asking?
A sunbeam.

queerness
What is it that is very queer about flowers?
They shoot before they have pistils.

questions
To what question can you never answer "yes"?
"Are you asleep?"

How would you define a questionnaire?
Someone who will inherit an inquiry.

queues
Where are you most likely to find a queue?
In a Chinese billiards parlor.

quiches
If your Aunt Matilda puts arsenic in her next quiche what does it become?
The quiche of death.

quiet
What is quiet when alive and noisy when dead?
A leaf.

quips
What could you say of those quips on late-hour talk shows?
They're just quips that pass in the night!

quotas
What is a quota?
Someone who is always quoting.

Q. It **runs** up the hill
And down the hill,
But in spite of all,
It still stands still.

A. A road.

R

Why is the letter R indispensable to friendship?
Because without it your friends would be fiends.

rabbi

What did the synagogue give the rabbi in appreciation of his years of service?
His own car and shofar.

rabbits

Why do rabbits have shiny noses?
Because their powder puffs are at the wrong end.

What did the rabbit say to the skunk?
"My scent is spoor but mine own."

Why is a rabbit the luckiest animal in the world?
Because it has four rabbit's feet.

What is the difference between a crazy rabbit and a counterfeit dollar?
One is a mad bunny and the other is bad money.

How can you catch a wild rabbit?
Throw him a bunch of carrots. All those tops will make him dizzy.

What did the boy rabbit reply when the father rabbit asked, "Can you keep my daughter in the manner to which she has been accustomed?"
"Oh yes, sir! When I marry her, I'll have the doe!"

What is a Welsh rabbit?
A girl from Wales who works in a bunny club.

races

If a woman is born in Greece, grows up in Turkey, and dies in the Texas
Panhandle, what is she?
Dead.

racing

Why is horse racing a necessity?
Because it is a matter of course.

What is the difference between horse racing and going to church?
One makes you bet and the other makes you better.

railroads

What did one railroad car say to the other?
"Let's get hitched."

"Railroad Crossing, Watch Out For Cars." Can you spell it without any *R*'s?
I-T!

rain

Why did the baseball team hope the rain would keep up?
So that it wouldn't come down.

What goes up when the rain comes down?
Umbrellas.

How can you tell if it rained cats and dogs last night?
You'll probably step in a poodle.

What is worse than raining cats and dogs?
Hailing taxis.

What is the difference between a cloud of rain and a spanked child?
One pours with rain and the other roars with pain.

After the rain falls, when does it rise again?
In dew time.

raindrops

What did the big raindrop say to the little raindrop?
"My plop is bigger than your plop!"

raising

What is the best way to raise turnips?
Take hold of the tops and pull.

ranchers
What did the Australian sheep rancher say to his wholesaler?
"Botany wool lately?"

Ranger, the Lone
What is the Lone Ranger's first name?
The.

When the Lone Ranger isn't out chasing bad guys, where can you usually find him?
In a bank, arranging loans.

reading
How should the following be read?
Yy u r yy u b
I c u r yy 4 me.
Too wise you are,
Too wise you be;
I see you are
Too wise for me.

red
What's red all day and goes up and down?
A. A sunburned elevator operator.
B. The Moscow Stock Exchange.

Red within and red without,
Four corners 'round about?
A brick.

What is red and blue
And purple and green?
No one can reach it,
Not even a queen?
A rainbow.

referee
Why are baseball umpires like chickens?
They both have foul mouths.

refrigerators
What would you do if your refrigerator started running?
Go chase it.

How did the housewife know that there had been an elephant in her refrigerator?
She saw his footprints in the butter.

relations

What relation is a loaf of bread to a television set?
The mother—bread being a necessity, a television being an invention, and necessity being the mother of invention.

If your uncle's sister is not your aunt, what relation is she to you?
Your mother.

Which of your parents is your nearest relation?
Your mother, of course. The other is farther.

While two brothers, Arthur and Ernie, were out for a walk they saw four fair-haired children approaching. "I must speak to the kids," said Arthur. "After all, they're my nieces and nephews." "Go ahead," said Ernie. "Since I don't have any nieces or nephews, I'll just keep walking." How could Ernie say that?
They were Ernie's children!

religion

Which birds are religious?
Birds of pray.

What is the policy of religion?
Fire insurance.

Which insect is the most religious?
A praying mantis.

reporters

Under what circumstances are a newpaper reporter and a builder equally likely to fail?
When they put up stories without foundations.

requirements

What is it we all require, we all give, we occasionally ask for, but very seldom take?
Advice.

If you want to increase church attendance, what is the first thing you require?
The choir loft.

resolutions

When you go to bed, why are your shoes like most good resolutions?
Because they are put off until the next day.

Why is a resolution like a girl fainting on the dance floor?
Because it ought to be carried out.

Why is a resolution like a mirror?
Because it is so easily broken.

responsibility
What one thing is most likely to reduce your responsibility?
A wad of gum.

restlessness
Why is the ocean so restless?
It could hardly rest easy with so many rocks in its bed!

restoring
What is the best way to restore a wig?
Take it back.

returning
What is it that we often return but never borrow?
Thanks.

riddles
What is the difference between compiling a dictionary of riddles and letting Turkish potentates ride on your merry-go-round?
One causes busy days and the other causes dizzy beys.

What is the difference between playing with riddles and playing with nurses?
One is a word game and the other is a ward game.

What is the difference between a riddle and an aunt that squints?
One is a query with an answer and the other an aunt, sir, with a queer eye.

riders
Why is a horseback rider like a cloud?
Because they both hold the reins.

riding
What rides in a car
Over hills and over hollows,
Going always too far
While it eats but never swallows?
Rust.

rifles
Why is a rifle like a lazy worker?
Because they can both get fired.

right
What can be right but never wrong?
An angle.

rings
What is a ring?
A hole with a rim around it.

What is it that people ring yet it is never heard?
The bathtub.

rivers

What are the little rivers called that run into the Nile?
The juveniles.

Why is a river a handy place for getting money?
Because there is a bank on either side.

roasts

Which is better, getting the girl of your choice or a roast of beef?
A roast of beef, since nothing is better than getting the girl and a roast of beef is much better than nothing.

robbers

What is the first thing a robber heads for in a music store?
The lute.

robbery

What kind of robbery is not dangerous?
A safe robbery.

rocks

If a rock isn't ugly, what do you call it?
Gneiss.

What is big and red and eats rocks?
A big red rock eater.

romance

How would you cook up a romance with a sailor?
You might start with a pinch of salt.

roofs

What roof covers the noisiest tenant?
The roof of your mouth.

Why did the fat girl sit on the roof?
She had heard that the treats were on the house.

rooms

What is the largest room in the world?
Room for improvement.

Why is a roomful of married people empty?
Because there isn't a single person in it.

What is the smallest room in the world?
The mushroom.

roosters

The Chinese ask, "What is like a big rooster? When it sees a visitor it makes a bow."
A teapot.

Why did the rooster refuse to fight?
Because it was really chicken.

How do you stop a rooster from crowing early on Sunday morning?
Eat it Saturday night.

ropes

When is a rope like a child at school?
When it is taut.

Why did the big rope scold the little rope?
Because it was knotty.

roses

Why is a distant rose like a distant woman?
Because you can't get attar.

To show his affection, a boy will often send a girl a single red rose. Why would he be better off sending her tulips?
Because tulips are better than one.

How do you clean a dirty rose?
Give it a flower shower.

What is the difference between a rose and a nose?
It is polite to pick a rose.

round

What's round and black and goes "Hic, hic, hic"?
A cracked Hickory Dickory Dock record.

What is round at both ends and high in the middle?
Ohio.

Round as a biscuit,
Busy as a bee,
Prettiest little thing
I ever did see.
A watch.

Round as an apple,
Yellow as gold,
With more things in it
Than you're years old.
A pumpkin.

As round as pies,
And flat as chips,
I've got four eyes
But have no hips.
A button.

Round as a biscuit,
Deep as a cup,
All the great rivers
Can't fill it up.
A strainer.

rowing

Who is it that rows quickly with four oars but never comes out from under his own roof?
The sea turtle.

For what profession are the members of a college rowing crew best suited?
For dentistry, because they have a good pull.

rudders

When the family goes sailing, why should Father always handle the rudder?
Because he can take stern measures.

What is the difference between a rudder and a butcher?
A rudder steers the way and a butcher weighs the steer.

rudeness

Why is it rude to whisper?
Because it is not aloud.

Which is the rudest bird?
The mockingbird.

rugs

Why is a dirty rug like a bad boy?
Because both need beating.

What did the rug say to the floor?
"Don't move—I have you covered!"

rulers
Why did the princess take a ruler to bed with her?
To see how long she slept.

running
What will run up a hill faster than it will run down?
Fire.

What sort of day would be good for running for a cup?
A muggy day.

The faster you run the harder I am to catch. What am I?
Your breath.

What is always running but never gets anywhere?
A clock.

It runs up the hill
And down the hill,
But in spite of all,
It still stands still.
A road.

What can run and whistle, but can't walk or talk?
A locomotive.

What runs to sea, has eyes, yet can't see?
The Mississippi River.

It runs and runs
And never tires,
Down and down
And never up.
A river.

What never runs in but forever runs out?
Time.

Who was the best runner in the Bible?
Adam. He came first in the human race.

Russians
Why did the Russians invent brainwashing?
So many of their people had dirty minds.

Q. Why did the **scientist**
disconnect his doorbell?

A. Because he wanted
to win the Nobel Prize.

SSSSSSS

S
Why is the letter S like thunder?
It makes our cream sour cream.

Why is the letter S like a sewing machine?
Because it makes needles needless.

Sadat
Why were the Israelis suspicious of Sadat?
They felt Egypt them.

saddles
What kind of saddle is best—one with a horn or one without?
If there isn't much traffic around, you probably won't need a horn.

Sade, Marquis de
Why was the Marquis de Sade like a baseball player?
He was a switch hurter.

sailboats
On a sailboat, what do you call that piece of wood that sticks out from the mast
and has the sail fastened to it?
That's the bough of the ship.

sailing
Why is sailing like writing graffiti?
It's a crewed business.

sailors

When is a sailor like a beach?
When he is ashore.

Why are Russian sailors like horses?
Because they are prone to pink aye.

Why should a sailor be a good pugilist?
Because he is always boxing the compass.

Why are sailors on a leaking ship like tap dancers?
They depend on their pumps.

When is a sailor not a sailor?
When he is aloft.

salads

What did the salad say to the spoon and fork?
"You get me all mixed up."

salesmen

What did the slipper salesman say when he had spent his last and was on his uppers?
"Well, that's shoe business!"

Why is a dishonest cheese salesman the worst kind of criminal?
Only a jerk would milk his firm of expenses when none have been in curd.

salt

What did Lot do when his wife got turned into a block of salt?
He put her in the cellar.

What did the big saltcellar say to the little saltcellar?
"Let's shake on it!"

Samson

Why was Samson so upset?
Because he had been bald out.

sandpaper

What does a puppy say when it sits on sandpaper?
"Ruff!"

sandwich

What did one sandwich say to the other?
"You're full of bologna!"

Santa Claus

How does Santa Claus arrive in Africa?
Accompanied by jungle belles.

Why has Santa Claus taken up gardening?
Because he likes to hoe, hoe, hoe.

What did Santa say to his reindeer on Christmas Eve?
"You sleigh me!"

Why does Santa Claus always go down the chimney?
Because it soots him.

satisfaction
Where does satisfaction come from?
From a satisfactory.

saving
What has a soul that can't be saved?
A shoe.

saws
A man with his trousers rolled to the knee, his saw over his head.
A rooster.

sayings
What do we mean when we say, "It's raining cats and dogs"?
It's pelting.

scales
Why are scales like roadmaps?
Because they show the weigh.

scarfs
There is a big white scarf across the gate.
A snowdrift.

scholars
What kind of jokes does a scholar make?
Wisecracks.

schools
What do students like most to hear in school?
The bell to go home.

Why is an exclusive school for girls like a flower garden?
Because it's a place of haughty culture.

scientists
Why was the mad scientist in the old castle like the alcoholic cricket player in the locker room?
He kept his secret under his bat.

Why did the scientist disconnect his doorbell?
Because he wanted to win the Nobel Prize.

scissors

What did the scissors say to the barber?
"It won't be long now!"

Scotsmen

When is a Scotsman like a donkey?
When he walks by the banks and braes.

sculptors

How does a sculptor die?
He makes faces and busts.

seamstress

Why is a good seamstress like a good poet?
She knows how to turn the frays.

seas

How did the sailor know that there wasn't a man in the moon?
He had been to sea.

What sea is most traveled by clever people?
Brilliancy.

Who sails the seven seas and makes very good suits?
Sinbad the Tailor.

seasickness

Why are seasick passengers like a strong opposition in Congress?
Because they are opposed to every motion.

seasons

Which of the four seasons is the most literary?
Autumn, for then the leaves are turned and red.

secrets

Why should secrets never be told in a vegetable garden?
Because the potatoes have eyes, the corn has ears, and the beans stalk.

Why should you never confide a secret to your relatives?
Because blood will tell.

seeds

Why are seeds like gateposts?
Because they propagate.

seeing

What is always in front of you but you cannot see?
Your future.

When can you see through a friend?
When she has a pain in her stomach.

When did the blind man suddenly see?
When he took up a hammer and saw.

What can I see that you cannot?
The back of your head.

I see, I see,
Two miles over the sea,
A little blue man in a green boatee;
His shirt is lined with red.
A rainbow.

What two things are never seen at all?
The wind and love.

What is it that a man may often see but George Washington seldom saw and God Almighty never saw?
His equal.

What is it that is seen twice in every day and four times in every week yet only once in a year?
The vowel E.

What is it that you and every living person have seen but can never see again?
Yesterday.

senators

What is a senator?
A creature half man and half hoarse.

sentences

Who doesn't mind being interrupted in the middle of a sentence?
A convict.

sergeants

Why are army sergeants like dentists?
Because they are both good at drilling.

What is the best way to make sergeant?
Bring her flowers.

Seville
What are government workers called in Seville?
Seville servants.

sewing machines
What is the difference between a sewing machine and a kiss?
One sews seams nice and the other seems so nice.

sex
What is the first thing a farm boy learns about sex?
It's just one barn thing after another.

shadows
What can pass between you and the sun without making a shadow?
The wind.

sharks
Why shouldn't you worry about sharks that travel in pairs?
The thing to watch out for is the lone shark.

When was the shark shocked?
When it met the electric eel.

shaving
Who can shave many times a day and still have a beard?
The barber.

sheep
What would happen if you ordered roast sheep in a restaurant?
You might get lambasted.

sheets
What sheet can't be folded?
A sheet of ice.

ships
What kind of crew does a ghost ship have?
A skeleton crew.

What are the most difficult ships to conquer?
Hardships.

What is the difference between a beached ship and an airplane?
One grounds on the land and the other lands on the ground.

What is the last blow a defeated ship gives in battle?
She strikes her own flag.

shoes

Why do we buy shoes?
Because we can't get them for nothing.

Why was the little shoe so bad?
Its mother was a sneaker and its father was a loafer.

What did Mary's red shoes become when she stepped in the river?
Wet.

Why is a giant's shoe like a generous person?
Because it has a large sole.

How long is a shoe?
One foot long.

Who always goes to bed with his shoes on?
A horse.

Do you know how to shoe a horse?
Just wave a blanket at it!

Why does a smart man always put on his right shoe first?
It would be silly to put on the wrong shoe first.

What did the big shoe say to the little shoe?
"You'll do in a pinch."

shorthand

What should you do if you want to write shorthand?
Cut your fingers off.

showers

Why are heavy showers like heavy drinkers?
Because they usually begin with little drops.

Siamese

What do you call a Siamese businessman?
A Thaicoon.

sickness

What should you do to stop from getting sick the night before a trip?
Leave a day earlier.

sides

What has two sides and a thousand ribs?
A railroad track.

Which is the west side of a little boy's pants?
The side the son sets on.

How many sides has a pitcher?
Two—inside and outside.

sidewalks

Why are sidewalks in the winter like music?
Because if you don't C-sharp you will B-flat.

sight

What is never out of sight?
The letter S.

simpletons

What is the difference between a simpleton and a Welsh rarebit?
One is easy to cheat and the other is cheesy to eat.

sinks

Why is a sink like a gambler visiting a ranch?
It's there to clean the hands.

sisters

I have a little sister called Peep-Peep.
She wades in the water, deep, deep.
She climbs up the mountain, high, high.
Yet poor little sister has but one eye.
A star.

sitting

What sits on the stove without burning itself?
What sits on the table and is not ashamed?
What goes through a keyhole without pinching itself?
The sun.

size

Why does a woman's size not matter in lovemaking?
It is better to have loved a short girl than never to have loved a tall.

The size of a nut, it climbs the mountain and has no feet.
The snail.

skeletons

What is a skeleton?
Some bones with the people scraped off.

Why didn't the skeleton go to the dance?
Because it had nobody to go with.

What did it miss by not going?
A rattling good time!

Why didn't the skeleton cross the road?
It didn't have the guts.

skiers

If you knew an amateur skier who was leaving for Switzerland what is the best advice you could give him?
Do a slow Bern.

What happens when a novice skier makes the wrong assumption about the height of a cliff?
He jumps to contusions.

skiing

Why should you never ski on an empty stomach?
Because snow works much better.

skin

If you take off my skin, I won't cry, but you will!
An onion.

As I went down the country road,
I met old Granny Gray.
I ate her meat and sucked her blood
And threw her skin away.
A watermelon.

skin divers

What do you call a frightened skin diver?
Chicken of the sea.

skirts

Riddle, come riddle, you varlet;
Skirted round in scarlet,
Stone in the middle,
Stick in the tail,
Tell me this riddle
Without any fail
A cherry.

skunks

Why is the skunk actually popular with other animals?
He is their community scenter.

What do skunks have that no other animal has?
Baby skunks.

The mother skunk had two baby skunks—In and Out. When Out was in, In was out. One day, In went out and Out came in and the mother skunk sent Out out to send In in. How did Out find In?
Instinct.

How do you keep a skunk from smelling?
Give it nose plugs.

What do you get when you cross a skunk with an owl?
A bird that smells, but doesn't give a hoot.

skylarks

Why did the skylark fly over the wall?
Because it couldn't fly through it.

When is a skylark unlucky?
When the captain or co-pilot catches you at it.

sleep

Why couldn't Virginia sleep last night?
She had plugged her electric blanket into the toaster and kept popping out of bed.

What should you do if you're a light sleeper?
Sleep on a lamp.

Who sleeps legs up, head down?
A bat.

Why is a sleepy man like a carpet?
He must have his nap.

slight

What is long and slight,
Works in the light,
Has but one eye
And an awful bite?
A needle.

smell

What smells the most in a drugstore?
The nose.

Why do we sometimes say that a book smells?
Because it has faults on every odor page.

smooth

Runs as smooth as any rhyme,
Loves to fall but cannot climb?
Water.

When is a politician his smoothest?
In his oily days.

snails

What happens when two snails get into a fight?
They just slug it out.

snakes

Why is a snake the most careless animal in the world?
Because he even loses his skin.

What snake is good at math?
An adder.

sneezes

Where is a sneeze usually pointed?
Achoo!

What do you do when an elephant sneezes?
Get out of the way.

snow

Why is snow like a tree?
Because it leaves in the spring.

Why is snow easier to understand than any other sort of weather?
Because you can see the drift.

snowflakes

Where do snowflakes dance?
At a snowball.

Snow White

Who was Snow White's brother?
Egg White . . . get the yolk?

snooty

Which are the snootiest animals in the zoo?
Giraffes, because they look down on people.

soap

What is a soap opera?
Your daily bathos.

Why was the soap left on the dining room table?
So people could use it to wash down their food.

social life

Why did the India rubber man have a poor social life?
Every time he went to a party he made an S of himself.

How could his social life have been improved?
It would have been better if he had decided to go straight.

socks
> What did the sock say to the foot?
> *"You're putting me on!"*

Socrates
> How did Socrates get to Athens?
> *The stoic brought him.*

soirées
> If you decided to hold a political soirée how would you describe it?
> *A carafe tea occasion.*

soldiers
> Who are the shortest soldiers in the army?
> *The infantry, because they are foot soldiers.*

> What does a soldier have to be, to be buried with full military honors?
> *Dead.*

> Who is the greatest "Soldier of Fortune"?
> *Its publisher.*

songs
> What sort of song would a ghost sing?
> *A haunting melody.*

> Why do so many country and western songs fail to cheer us up?
> *The malady lingers on.*

sorcerers
> What is a good sorcerer called?
> *A charming fellow.*

sorceresses
> What is a nervous sorceress called?
> *A twitch.*

sound
> What travels at the speed of sound, but doesn't have legs, wings, or engines?
> *Your voice.*

soups
> What is a cannibal's favorite kind of soup?
> *One with plenty of body in it.*

spanking
> How did the boy feel after being spanked in the backyard?
> *Whacked out.*

spawning

How do fish manage to swim upstream to spawn?
They salmon their strength.

speakers

Why is a windy speaker like a whale?
Because he often rises to spout.

When does a public speaker steal lumber?
When he takes the floor.

spearing

How did the African chief challenge his brother in spear-throwing?
"Brother, can you spear a dime?"

speeches

Why is a long speech like a pine tree?
Because you can get bored from it.

spelling

How do you feel if you are being kept after school for bad spelling?
Spellbound.

Which is is easier to spell, fiddle-de-dee or fiddle-de-dum?
Fiddle-de-dee is spelled with more E's.

spendthrifts

What is the difference between a spendthrift and a feather bed?
One is hard up and the other soft down.

spiders

What did history's Robert the Bruce do after he watched the spider climbing up and down?
He invented the Yo-Yo.

What do you call two spiders who just got married?
Newlywebs.

spies

Where can I buy the equipment to become a spy?
At any snooper market.

Why are Communist secret agents like young capitalists?
Both are aspiring.

What did the male spy say to the female spy?
"Even though you have a code, I still cipher you."

spinning
It spins, but not cloth, yet when it works it weaves.
A top.

What does a young man mean when he says, "Let's go for a spin"?
It's a gambling term. It means he wants to flip you.

spinsters
Why did the two Scottish spinsters buy a sailboat?
They hoped that they'd find a monsoon.

sponges
Why is a loofah sponge the most popular kind?
All the world loves a loofah.

What is the difference between a sponge and a cheap night club?
A sponge drinks the water and the night club waters the drink.

spooks
What is the spooks' navy called?
The Ghost Guard.

Who usually represents spooks at a press conference?
Their spooksman.

spots
Out of Africa comes:
Who is that? Who is that? The spots are going; the spots are hiding. Who is that?
A leopard.

spring
What takes spring so long to pass?
It's a long march.

In spring I am gay
In handsome array,
In summer more clothing I wear;
When colder it grows,
I fling off my clothes,
And in winter quite naked appear.
A tree.

squirrels
Why is a squirrel like the world?
It's fur from one end to the other.

How do you catch a squirrel?
Climb up a tree and act like a nut.

stabbing

What is the difference between stabbing a man and killing a hog?
One is assaulting with intent to kill and the other is killing with intent to salt.

What is the difference between stabbing and stubbing?
It's the difference between a drip and a trip.

stable

What is the most widely accepted stable diet?
Hay.

What did Mary whisper to Joseph when the innkeeper offered them accommodation in the stable?
"Keep arguing. It's a stall!"

stamps

Why is a postage stamp like a very precise man?
Because they both stick to the letter.

When can 225 pounds go for a twenty-cent stamp?
When his wife sends him to get it.

standing

Why do audiences give performers standing ovations?
They feel that they have to rise to the occasion.

What gets lost every time you stand up?
Your lap.

In India, you get asked:
What stands up, night and day?
The horns on an ox.

Little Miss Nannycot, in a white petticoat and a red nose; the longer she stands the shorter she grows.
A candle.

staphylococcus

If your company is hit by an epidemic of staphylococcus infection what is the first thing to do?
Put someone in charge of staph relations.

starlets

What did the starlet tell the producer after her first visit to his apartment?
"I didn't like the champagne—but I just loved the baubles."

stars

When you visit Hollywood, where can you always be sure of seeing lots of stars?
In the Milky Way.

What is behind every gold star?
A police officer.

states

What is the happiest state in the Union?
Maryland.

Which state produces the most marriages?
The state of matrimony.

Statue of Liberty, the

Why does the Statue of Liberty stand in New York harbor?
Because she can't sit down.

Why does Liberty always wear the same clothes?
Because she only has one Jersey to her back.

staying

Go down. Here we stay.
Come up. Let's away!
An anchor.

steaks

What did the steak say to the plate?
"Pleased to meat you."

stealing

If you ever steal money what is the first thing you should do?
Wash it. Grime doesn't pay.

steamrollers

Why did it take so long for the steamroller to be invented?
It's hard stuff to roll.

What happened to the woman who was run over by the steamroller?
She was in the hospital for quite a stretch.

steel

What is the head of a steel corporation called?
A magnet.

What is the motto of the Krupp steel barons?
Ingot We Trust.

steeples

If a man happened to be on a steeple 300 feet high with a goose and the
ladder was taken away, how could he get down?
Pluck the goose.

steps

What steps should you take when you first see a giant?
Giant steps.

What are the first steps to take to overcome communism?
The Russian steppes.

stew

What is the real nature of lamb stew?
Much ado about mutton.

stewardesses

Why are there so few married airline stewardesses?
Who'd want to marry a plane woman?

sticks

Why is a good walking stick so hard to find?
It has a poor sense of direction.

How many sticks go into the building of a crow's nest?
None—they are all carried.

stoats

What happened when two American stoats got married?
They became the United Stoats of America.

stockings

Why do stockings have holes in them?
So that you can get your feet in.

stocks

Why did the stock promoter buy a dairy farm?
He was tired of milking the public.

stones

Guess a riddle now you must:
Stone is fire, and fire is dust,
Black is red, and red is white—
Come and view the wondrous sight.
Coal.

stores

How is a bookstore like a boat?
They both have sales.

storks

Why is the stork associated with birth?
Because we all come into this world stork naked.

We all know where babies come from but where do storks come from?
The stork market.

What does a stork do when it stands on one foot?
It lifts up the other.

straight
Who was the straightest man in the Bible?
Joseph. Pharaoh made a ruler of him.

strawberries
Why was the little strawberry worried?
His mom and dad were in a jam.

streetcars
Why are more and more city councils deciding to do away with streetcars?
They are finding that it is just one tram thing after another.

strength
What was the greatest feat of strength ever performed?
Wheeling, West Virginia.

The ancient Greeks asked:
"What is strongest?"
Their answer:
"Love." They reasoned that while iron is strong, the blacksmith can bend it.
Yet love can overcome the blacksmith.

What is the best food to eat if you want to be strong?
Mussels.

strings
What is the black string in the path?
A procession of ants.

stuffiness
Why did it get so stuffy as the party went on last night?
The air conditioner only ventilate.

stupidity
What kind of fish is the most stupid?
A simple salmon.

subways
What is the subway in New York called?
The burrow of Manhattan.

success
Why was Wolfgang Amadeus Mozart so successful?
He was an opera-tunist.

suds
Name two ways of getting lots of suds.
Use a soap (or detergent)—or head for the nearest bar!

sugar
Why do farmers give sugar to their sick pigs?
So that they will get sugar-cured hams.

sugar daddies
What's another name for a sugar daddy?
A lolly pop.

suits
What occupation suits everybody?
A tailor.

What is the best pattern for a banker's suit?
Checks.

Sullivan, John L.
Who was the last man to box John L. Sullivan?
The undertaker.

summer
How did Simon Legree spend his summer?
Serfing.

How is it that summer goes so quickly?
Because there is so often an evening mist.

sun
What is the difference between a rising sun and a setting sun?
The whole world.

sunbathers
What is the difference between a sunbather and someone who lives in the Sahara?
One gets tanned by the sun and the other gets sand by the ton.

sunburns
What do you call a sunburn on your stomach?
A pot roast.

Sunday
Why is Sunday the strongest day?
Because it isn't a weekday.

Superman
Who was Superman?
The founder of the Campbell Soup Company.

supermarkets
What is the difference between a woman in a supermarket and the tide?
One shops at the store and the other stops at the shore.

surgeons
What did the surgeon say to the patient after the operation?
"That will be enough out of you!"

suspenders
Why do firemen wear red suspenders?
To keep their pants up. *

swamps
Why should you never argue about the ownership of a swamp?
It really doesn't matter; ooze.

Sweden
Why doesn't Sweden export cattle?
Because she wants to keep her Stockholm.

sweets
What sort of sweets are good for your teeth?
Gums.

swimming
Why should you never swim on an empty stomach?
It's easier to swim in water.

What does a fish do before it learns to swim?
Roe.

What does the Bible tell us is the best way to teach children to swim?
Cast thy brood upon the waters.

What is the best way to overcome the feeling that swimming is for the birds?
Take a duck in the water.

What old saying prompts long-distance swimmers to grease themselves before
plunging into cold waters?
The oily bird catches the warm.

switches
What did the light switch say to the new maid?
"Boy, do you turn me on!"

---

* This well-known riddle has many relatives. Suspenders vary in color, their users in occupation. The
logic of the answer is more apparent for firemen, however. It would be inadvisable for a person so
dangerously occupied to have a belt on the job.

syllables

What word is made shorter by adding a syllable to it?
Short.

What word of only three syllables contains in it twenty-six letters?
Alphabet.

sympathy

Where can you always find sympathy?
In the dictionary.

*Q. I went out walking one day and met three beggars. To the first I gave ten cents, to the second I also gave ten cents, and to the third I gave only five. Now, what **time** of day was it?*

tttt tt tt

A. A quarter to three.

T

In hockey, what makes the letter *T* so important to a stick handler?
Because without it, he would be a sick handler.

Why do you need the letter *T* to set one of the heavenly bodies in motion?
Because it will make a star start.

Why is an island like the letter *T*?
Because it is in the midst of water.

tables

What table do we use almost every day, yet it really doesn't have a leg to stand on?
The multiplication table.

tailors

Why are good tailors so temperamental?
They are always having fits.

How should you refer to a tailor when you don't remember his name?
As Mr. So-and-So.

What is the difference between a tailor and a stable boy?
One mends a tear and the other tends a mare.

tails

Why is the end of a dog's tail like the heart of a tree?
Because it is farthest from the bark.

In India, they pose this one:
Long is its tail
(But it's not a squirrel).
It sometimes has horns
(But it's not a cow).
It flies in the sky
(But it's not a bird).
What is it?
A kite.

What animal eats with its tail?
They all do. None of them can remove their tails to eat.

Old Mother Twitchit had but one eye
And a long tail which she let fly,
And every time she went over a gap,
She left a bit of her tail in a trap.
A needle and thread in sewing.

What did the pig say when the farmer caught him by the tail?
"This is the end of me."

taking

The more you take from it,
The larger it gets.
A hole.

Movies are shot in brief numbered sections or "takes." Which take can be the most expensive for the director?
Take Five. If he doesn't watch it, when it is announced everyone leaves for coffee!

talking

What has a tongue, but never talks?
A shoe.

Why are tongue-lashings usually ineffective?
The string keeps slipping off.

tallness

What is the tallest building in town?
The library. It has the most stories.

Why does a tall man eat less than a short one?
He makes a little go a long way.

What is taller sitting than standing?
A dog.

How can you make a tall man short?
Borrow money from him.

Not very tall,
Ears like a mule,
Tail like a cotton ball,
Runs like a fool.
A rabbit.

How do you know that tall people are lazier than short people?
Because they lie longer in bed.

tapes
What did the tape say to the paper?
"Stick with me and I'll see what I can glue for you."

Do recording tapes only come in reels?
No, they come in jigs and waltzes as well.

taps
Why is a leaky tap like a coward?
Because it keeps running.

Why do army buglers play taps at sundown?
Because their instruments have been taken away for the night.

Tarzan
What is Tarzan saying each time he beats his chest?
Nothing. He is just coughing.

Who is Tarzan's favorite folk singer?
Harry Elephanté.

What does Tarzan sing at Christmas time?
Jungle Bells.

taxi drivers
Why should a taxi driver be brave?
Because none but the brave deserve the fare.

What is the most common ailment among taxi drivers?
A hacking cough.

tea
What is the proper thing to wear to a tea party?
A T-shirt would be cozy.

What did the young girl say when she detected an aphrodisiac in her tea?
"I think that's not tea!"

Why is the cost of tea so high?
Because we must pay a steep price.

Many people like to sip Chinese tea slowly, but what about the rest?
Samovar friends prefer Russian.

Why should you go to bed after drinking tea?
Because when T is gone, night is nigh.

teachers
Why are teachers rather special?
Because they are usually in a class of their own.

What did the young male teacher whisper to the girl in charge of assigning pupils?
"Save the less dense for me!"

What is the difference between a teacher and a train?
The teacher says, "Spit out that gum!" and the train says, "Chew, chew, chew."

What is the difference between a schoolteacher and a train's conductor?
One trains the mind and the other minds the train.

When a teacher closes her eyes, why should she remind you of an empty classroom?
Because there are no pupils to see.

What is the difference between a teacher and a supermarket cashier?
One tills the mind while the other minds the till.

teaspoons
What is a teaspoon?
Lovemaking on the golf course.

teeth
What did one tooth say to the other tooth?
"The dentist is taking me out tonight!"

Why do you forget a tooth after it is pulled?
Because it has gone right out of your head.

What has sharp teeth but no mouth?
A saw.

How can you have a new set of teeth inserted free of charge?
Kick a bulldog.

What are the last teeth you get called?
False.

telegrams
Why is it useless to send a telegram to Washington?
Because he's dead.

telegraph
If two Texas telegraph operators were married, what would they become?
A Western Union.

telephone
How do you telephone from a streetcar?
It's easy—the streetcar has wheels.

telephoning
Why is waiting on the telephone like doing a trapeze act?
Because you have to hang on.

television
After the Joneses had bought their first television set, why did they turn it on only once?
They didn't know how to turn it off.

What sort of people want to go on television?
Those who like being in the picture.

What is the most popular television quiz program in Ireland?
Dublin or Nothing.

Why did Charlie sit in front of the television set with milk and sugar?
He had heard that there was going to be a new serial.

What was the first Chinese television show called?
Tibet Your Life.

tellers
Why is a bank teller always well informed?
Because he is continually taking notes.

What was the old-fashioned male bank manager's complaint when he had to work with his first female teller?
"You can teller some things, but you can't teller much!"

temper
When is it a good thing to lose your temper?
When it's a bad one.

Why are you like two people when you lose your temper?
Because you are beside yourself.

What is the superlative of temper?
Tempest.

Tennessee

What did Tennessee?
She saw what Arkansas.

tennis

Where is tennis mentioned in the Bible?
Where Joseph served in Pharaoh's court.

tennis players

What is the difference between a strong tennis player and a bully?
One smashes the ball and the other bashes the small.

Why is a champion tennis player like a king?
Because he rules the court.

termites

What did the termite say to the tree?
"It was nice gnawing you!"

theaters

What is the coldest place in a theater?
Z row.

What is the difference between the manager of a theater and a sailor?
A sailor likes to see a lighthouse and the manager doesn't.

theology

To what do theologians devote most of their time?
Debating the origin of the specious.

thrift

Why are goalkeepers thrifty?
Because saving is their job.

throwing

When would it make sense to throw sliced tomatoes and lettuce around the room?
When you want a tossed salad.

Where are throw rugs most desirable?
In wrestling.

thunder

What is the difference between thunder and a lion's toothache?
One may cause it to pour with rain and the other may cause it to roar with pain.

tickling

A boy said to his sister, "I saw something at the circus that would tickle you."

"Oh," she asked, "was it a monkey?" "No." "Was it a dancing bear?" "No. It was—"?
A straw.

ties

What did the tie say to the hat?
"Don't just hang around, go on ahead."

Where are the most attractive ties to be found?
In Thailand.

tigers

If there was a tiger on your right side, a lion on your left side, and in front and back of you were wild elephants, what should you do?
Get off the merry-go-round.

tightrope walkers

Why are tightrope walkers like bookkeepers?
Because they know how to balance.

Why did the tightrope walker decide to give up?
Because his performance began to fall off.

time

Why does time fly so fast?
Because so many people are trying to kill it.

If you saw a long snake and a short snake waking up from their naps, what time would it be?
Time to run.

What time is it when a hippopotamus sits on a chair?
Time to get a new chair.

If twenty dogs run after one dog, what time is it?
Twenty after one.

What animal keeps the best time?
A watch dog.

I went out walking one day and met three beggars. To the first I gave ten cents, to the second I also gave ten cents, and to the third I gave only five. Now, what time of day was it?
A quarter to three.

What's always behind time?
The back of a clock.

What is the best way to make time go quickly?
Use the spur of the moment.

tiny
> Tiny as a mouse,
> Like a lion it guards the house.
> *A key.*

tired
> Why are people always tired on the first day of April?
> *Because they've just had a thirty-one-day March.*

titles
> What foreign letter is an English title?
> *The Dutch S.*

toasts
> What did the American reply when the Norwegian raised his glass and cried "Skoal!"?
> *"Of course it is. It has ice in it."*

toes
> What should you do if your toe falls off?
> *Get to the doctor quickly—call a toe truck.*

> What did the big toe say to the little toes?
> *"There's a big heel following us."*

tongues
> What lies around all night with its tongue hanging out?
> *A shoe.*

> Why is the root of the tongue like a dejected man?
> *Because it's down in the mouth.*

toothpaste
> When do Scotsmen use toothpaste?
> *When their teeth are loose.*

> What happens to people who don't know toothpaste from putty?
> *All their windows fall out.*

touch
> Why does your sense of touch suffer when you are ill?
> *Because you don't feel well.*

> What can you hold without touching it?
> *Your tongue.*

> Can two people stand just two inches apart and still not be able to touch each other?
> *Yes. Shut the door between them.*

Toulouse-Lautrec
How did the French girl persuade artist Toulouse-Lautrec to go home with her?
"What have you got, Toulouse?"

toupees
What happened when the French horn player's toupee fell into his instrument?
He spent the rest of the evening blowing his top.

tourists
What is the first thing a tourist learns in Moscow?
That Lenin's tomb is a Communist plot.

Tower of Babel, the
What was the distinguishing feature of the Tower of Babel?
It was a din of iniquity.

tracks
What goes around the house and makes but one track?
A wheelbarrow.

What goes around the house and doesn't make a track?
The wind.

trains
How do you find a missing train?
Just follow its tracks.

What holds up a train?
Bad men.

Why can't a train sit down?
Because it has a tender behind.

Why is a train like a bed bug?
They both run over sleepers.

How do trains hear?
Through their engineers.

How can you make sure that the trains are running on time?
Just before one comes in, put your watch on the tracks.

trampolines
Why is a trampoline act a tricky way of earning a living?
Because it's full of ups and downs.

transposing
Part of a foot with judgment transpose,

And the answer you'll find just under your nose.
Inch = chin.

traps
Why is a steel trap like a bad cold?
Because it is catching.

travel
When are babies traveling abroad?
When going to Brest.

We travel much, yet prisoners are,
And close confined to boot.
We with the swiftest horse keep pace,
Yet always go on foot.
A pair of spurs.

What is it that travels over the fields and hills all day long and sits in a refrigerator at night?
Milk.

Me riddle, me riddle, me riddle, me ree
You tell me my riddle
I give you my fiddle.
I'll give you my fiddle
If you turn it back to me:
Under oak leaf, on gravel, I travel.
The ant.

What can travel around the world and still stay in one corner?
A postage stamp.

travel agents
What do you call a travel agent who flirts?
A wherewolf.

travelers
Why did the first-time traveler stand on his head when he came to Immigration?
Because some idiot had stuck in his passport photograph upside down.

trees
What do you need when your tree has a flat?
A lumberjack.

Which trees do hands grow in?
Palm trees.

What tree is the oldest?
The elder.

How can you tell a dogwood tree from a pine tree?
By its bark.

What did the lumberjack say when the tree fell on him?
"It looks like the oak's on me!"

How does an elephant get down from a tree?
It sits on a leaf and waits for fall.

Why is a tree surgeon like a famous actor?
He is always taking boughs.

trembling
I tremble with each breath of air,
And yet can heaviest burdens bear.
Water.

tricks
What do you have to know to teach an old dog new tricks?
More than the dog.

troops
If you are an army general should you always spread out your troops?
Sometimes deploy works.

trousers
How did the telegraph clerk explain the repair to his trousers?
"Detail is covered by dispatch."

Why are all trousers too short?
Because everyone's legs stick out two feet.

truant officers
How does a truant officer justify his job?
Necessity is the mother of detention.

trumpets
Why are three couples out walking like a toy trumpet?
Because they go two, two, two.

trunks
Why do elephants need trunks?
Because they don't have glove compartments.

What has a trunk but needs no key?
An elephant.

Why do dogs always head for the nearest trunk?
Because tree's company.

trusses

What is the truss-wearer's philosophy?
Into every life a little strain must fall.

truth

How can a person tell the naked truth?
By exposing the bare facts.

tubes

What did one tube of glue say to the other tube of glue?
"Tubes like us have to stick together."

turkeys

What happens when you cross a turkey and a centipede?
Everybody gets drumsticks at Thanksgiving.

Why is a turkey like a ghost?
Because it's always a-gobblin'.

What did the turkey say before it was roasted?
"Boy, am I stuffed!"

Where do all good turkeys go when they die?
To oven.

Why is the turkey a fashionable bird?
Because he always appears well dressed for dinner.

Turks

Why are the Turks so noisy?
They believe you should always salaam the door.

turning

What turns, but never moves?
Milk.

Turpin, Dick

For what was Dick Turpin, the highwayman, famous?
He was one of the first causes of traffic holdups.

After years of stopping travelers at a fork in the roads and crying, "Fork over!",
of what did Dick Turpin die?
Too much Turpintine.

turtles
In the fable of the race between the turtle and the rabbit, by how much did the turtle win?
By a hare.

Tussaud, Madame
Why should you protect your rear when visiting Madame Tussaud's?
Because you might get wax on your bottom!

twins
Why is a woman with new twins like a soldier on guard duty?
Because she marches up and down with loaded arms.

tying
Tie it and it walks,
Unfasten it and it stops.
Your shoe.

Q. What kind of **umbrella** does a Welshman carry when it is raining?

A. A wet one!

uuuuu

U

Why is the letter *U* important to your happiness?
Because you can't have fun without it.

Why are U-turns usually illegal?
They cause confusion in the herd.

ugliness

My first's an ugly insect.
My second, an ugly brute.
My whole's an ugly phantom
Which cannot please or suit.
Bugbear.

umbrellas

What kind of umbrella does a Welshman carry when it is raining?
A wet one!

Three children and a rather large puppy were crowded under one umbrella but none of them got wet. Why not?
It wasn't raining.

What did the umbrella say to the scarf?
"You go on ahead—I'll cover you."

umpires
Why did the German team cheer when the referee from London slipped in the mud?
They were delighted to see the fall of the British umpire.

undertakers
How can you tell an undertaker?
By his grave manner.

Where does an undertaker conduct his business?
In the box office.

unfairness
Which is the unfairest of all nations?
Discrimination.

unions
What is a representative of the Waiters' Union called?
A chop steward.

When is a marriage called a union?
When a striking girl gets married.

United States, the
Why is a healthy child like the United States?
Because it has a good constitution.

unlawful
What is the difference between unlawful and illegal?
One is against the law and the other is a sick bird.

unpleasant
What are the most unpleasant things for you to keep on hand?
Handcuffs.

up
What is it that goes up and never goes down?
Your age.

upsetting
Why should you never upset a cannibal?
Because if you do you might find yourself in hot water.

upside down
When should you address a letter upside down?
When you're sending it to Australia.

What happens when geese fly upside down?
They quack up.

use

Use me well and I am everybody. Scratch my back and I am nobody. What am I?
A mirror.

What is it that belongs to you but others use it more than you do?
Your name.

You use it between your head and your toes.
The more it works, the thinner it grows.
A bar of soap.

What part of a watch was used before by someone else?
The second hand.

usefulness

What is most useful when it is used up?
An umbrella.

utensils

My first part is a kitchen utensil.
My second is a big body of water.
My whole is a well-known flower.
Pansy.

*Q. What is the first rule a student **veterinarian** learns?*

A. Feed a colt and starve a beaver.

V

How is the letter V of help to a tourist lost in the Bronx?
He can always ask, "Where do V go from here?"

When does a V make a woman seem more attractive to men?
When it's in her neckline.

values

How can you best learn the value of money?
By trying to borrow some.

What increases its value one half when turned upside down?
The figure 6.

What valuable thing that he never really had and never will have can a man give to a woman?
A husband.

What is the moral value in selling all your gold?
You get rid of your gilt.

vampires

Why do vampires live in coffins?
Because the rent is low.

What did the polite vampire say to his dentist after being treated?
"Fangs very much!"

Why are vampires really simple-minded?
Because they are known to be suckers.

Why can't vampires start a baseball game in the afternoon?
Because the bats don't come out until night.

Vatican, the
What is the Pope's role in the Vatican?
He is the soul proprietor.

What is the telephone number for the Vatican?
Vat 69.

vaults
What is kept in an air-conditioned vault?
Cold cash.

Where is the best vault in Europe?
In Poland. You should see the Pole vault!

vegetables
What vegetable is measured like diamonds?
Carrots.

What vegetable hurts when you step on it?
Corn.

With what vegetable can you throw away the outside, cook the inside, eat the outside, and throw away the inside?
Corn.

What vegetable is never welcome on board a ship?
A leek.

Which vegetable has the most money in it?
The mint.

What vegetable do you find in big crowds?
Squash.

What two vegetables' names begin and end with the same two letters in the same order?
Tomato and onion.

vehicles
When does a bed become a vehicle?
When it is a little buggy.

My first part is a vehicle.
My second part is a preposition.
My whole is a cozy part of a ship.
Cabin.

My first part is a vehicle.
My second is what the United States is.
My whole is a flower.
Carnation.

verbs
When are teeth like verbs?
When they are regular, irregular, or defective.

Vesuvius, Mount
Why is Mount Vesuvius like an irritable person?
Because from time to time it blows its top.

veterinarians
What is the first rule a student veterinarian learns?
Feed a colt and starve a beaver.

Vikings
How do you talk to a Viking?
By Norse Code.

vines
What vine does beef grow on?
The bovine.

violinists
What is the difference between a pretty violinist and a sad spinster?
The violinist never lost her bow.

violins
How can you ask a doctor of divinity, in one word, to play a violin?
"Fiddle-dee-dee!"

What did the violin say to the harp?
"May I string along with you?"

visas
From what is the word "visa" derived?
From the assurance "Visa friendly people."

Why should you not worry if you are arrested for trying to get into Russia without your visa?
It's a borderline case.

visibility

What is visible only in winter?
Your breath.

visits

How do you know that elephants will always stay for a long time when they come to visit?
Because they bring their trunks.

voices

What is the difference between a man with an unnatural voice and a woman with unnatural teeth?
One has a falsetto voice and the other has a false set o' teeth.

volcanoes

What is a volcano?
A mountain with hiccups.

What is the volcano's favorite song?
"Lava, Come Back to Me."

volts

After whom was the electric volt named?
Voltaire—a shocking person.

vortex

What is a vortex?
The cost of conflict.

votes

Why is a vote in Congress like a cold?
Because sometimes the ayes have it and sometimes the noes.

vowels

There are only two words in our language in which the five vowels follow in successive order. Which are they?
Facetious and abstemious.

Is there another word in the English language that contains all the vowels?
Unquestionably.

Q. In what way is a **wedding** *like a game of cards?*

A. A woman has a heart, a man takes it with a diamond, and after that her hand is his.

W

Why is W the nastiest letter?
Because it always makes ill will.

waiters

Why are waiters always willing to learn?
Because they are ready to take tips from people.

Why is a waiter like a race horse?
Because he runs for cups, plates, and steaks.

Why did the waiter look grumpy?
Because he had a chip on his shoulder.

What is the difference between an eager waiter and an angry goat?
One keeps passing the butter and the other keeps butting the passer.

Why are waiters good at multiplication?
Because they know their tables.

Wales, Prince of

What is the difference between the Prince of Wales and the water in a fountain?
One is heir to the throne and the other is thrown to the air.

walking

When walking through a field of wheat
I picked up something good to eat.
'Twas neither fish, flesh, fowl, nor bone.
I kept it till it ran alone.
An egg.

It walks east, west, north, and south,
Has a tongue, but nary a mouth.
A shoe.

Who walks with three legs and has four eyes?
An old man with his cane and glasses.

I walk all day through rain and snow,
I scuff through sleet and hail,
I sleep a-standing on my head,
And you rhyme my name with snail.
A nail in a shoe.

Where is a walking stick mentioned in the Bible?
Where Eve presented Adam with a little Cain.

wallets

If you had only one dollar would you have less chance of losing it if you bought
a wallet?
Not at the price of wallets today!

walls

What did one wall say to the other wall?
"I'll meet you at the corner."

How can you jump higher than a four-foot wall?
Easily—a four-foot wall can't jump.

What is in the Great Wall of China that the Chinese never put there?
Cracks.

When is a wall like a fish?
When it is scaled.

Please explain to me
How this miracle can be:
I can throw an egg against the wall
And it will neither break nor fall.
The wall will not break.

war
What instrument of war does the earth resemble?
A revolver.

warmth
Why is a dog dressed more warmly in the summer than in the winter?
Because in the winter he wears a fur coat and in the summer he wears a fur coat and pants.

What is a good way to keep a house warm?
When you're painting it, give it two coats.

washing
I washed my hands in water that had never rained nor run,
I wiped my hands on silk that was neither woven nor spun.
This thing I did I did quite true,
But what it was is up to you!
I washed my hands in dew and wiped them on corn silk.

washing machines
Why should you never put elephants in your washing machine?
Their trunks will shrink.

Washington, George
What did George Washington say to his men before he crossed the Delaware?
"Get in the boat!"

Why do statues of George Washington always depict him standing?
Because he could never lie.

Why was George Washington buried at Mount Vernon?
Because he was dead.

wasps
If you get honey from a bee, what do you get from a wasp?
Waspberry jam.

watches
Why would you put bug spray on your watch?
To get rid of the ticks.

Why is a watch like a river?
Because it won't run long without winding.

Why should you always wear an old-fashioned watch when you are traveling in the desert?
Because every one has a spring in it.

watchmakers
What is the difference between a watchmaker and a prison warden?
One sells watches and the other watches cells.

water
What letter is a large body of water?
C.

What goes into the water, under the water, and through the water, but never gets wet?
An egg in a duck.

When will water stop running downhill?
When it gets to the bottom.

What goes over the water, under the water, and never touches the water?
A girl crossing a bridge with a pail of water on her head.

When is water most likely to escape?
When it is only half tide.

What is the best way to stop water from getting into your house?
Don't pay your water taxes.

How can you carry water in a strainer?
Freeze it.

What do you get when you pour hot water down a rabbit hole?
A hot, cross bunny!

Watergate
What did the Watergate affair teach politicians?
How to live by the law of the bungle.

watermelons
Why is there water in a watermelon?
Because it is planted in the spring.

Watt, James
What happened the day that James Watt saw steam coming from the kettle?
He almost blew his lid.

we
Can you spell *we* in two letters without using *w* or *e*?
U and I.

weasels
What happens when a train encounters a family of weasels?
It has to make a weasel stop.

weather
How can plumbers tell what the weather will be without using weather instruments?
By listening to the weather forecasts.

weatherman
As the wind intensity grew, why did the weatherman pull on boxing gloves?
He could see that it was going to come to blows.

weathor
What is weathor?
A bad spell of weather.

wedding
In what way is a wedding like a game of cards?
A woman has a heart, a man takes it with a diamond, and after that her hand is his. (In the days of the cavemen, he probably led with a club!)

weeds
Why do gardeners hate weeds?
Because if you give them an inch, they'll take a yard.

weeks
How many weeks in a year?
Forty-six, because six are Lent.

weight
What does a completely loaded cruise ship weigh when it leaves the harbor?
Its anchor.

What part of a fish weighs the most?
The scales.

What happens to people who try to lose weight?
They have a thin time of it.

You carry it everywhere you go and yet it does not seem to gain weight unless you become famous.
Your name.

What bird can lift the heaviest weight?
A crane.

wells
What can fall into a well without rippling the water?
The sunshine.

How can you find out how far to go with a well?
Ask Wells Fargo.

werewolves
What branch of the Armed Forces did the werewolf join?
The Hair Force.

Westminster Abbey
Why is Westminster Abbey like a fireplace?
Because it contains the ashes of the great.

wetness
The more it dries, the wetter it gets. What is it?
A towel.

whale hunters
What is the difference between a whale hunter and a happy dog?
One tags his whale and the other wags his tail.

whales
To a male whale, where is the most attractive spot he knows?
The bottom of the she.

In the Bible story, why did the whale finally let Jonah go?
He couldn't stomach him.

wheels
What happened when the wheel was invented?
It caused a revolution.

In India, they ask, "What is like a great wheel with twelve fiery, flaming spokes?"
The year with its twelve months.

What is big, has four wheels, and flies?
A garbage truck.

When are you most like an automobile wheel?
At night when you are tired.

whistling
Who is the oldest whistler in the world?
The wind.

white
What is black and white and green and black and white?
Two zebras fighting over a pickle.

White bird, featherless,
Flyin' out o' Paradise,
Flyin' over the sea and land,
Dyin' in my hand.
A snowflake.

The land is white,
The sea is black,
It'll take a good riddler
To answer me back!
Paper and ink.

White as snow and snow it isn't,
Green as grass and grass it isn't,
Red as blood and blood it isn't,
Black as tar and tar it isn't.
A blackberry: first, the white blossom, then the green berry that turns red, and, finally, when ripe it's black.

whole

From what can you take away the whole and still have some left?
The word wholesome.

whooping crane

If a whooping crane could be crossed with a pelican, what might you get?
A flying tuba.

Why does a whooping crane stand on one leg?
Because if it pulls them both up, it will fall down!

Wilde, Oscar

Why did Oscar Wilde have such a hairy time of it?
He was prematurely gay.

wills

What is the difference between your will and a man who has eaten as much as he can?
Your will is signed and dated and the man is dined and sated.

windows

What did the window say when the baseball hit it?
"I feel fine. My pane is gone!"

winds

What kind of wind would a hungry sailor prefer?
One that blows foul and chops about.

wines

When is wine like a pig's tooth?
When it is in a hogshead.

Why doesn't it matter what kind of wine you drink if it is snowing out?
Any port in a storm!

winter

Why is winter like a bad play?
Because it leaves us cold.

What is it that lives in the winter, dies in the summer, and grows with its roots upward?
An icicle.

What is the best way to kill time in the winter?
Sleigh it.

wires

When is the best time to send a friend a wire?
When he's at the end of his rope.

Why should wire be used to train string beans?
So that they won't be too stringy.

wit

What happens if a television comedian suddenly loses his wits?
He usually hires some more.

When is wit a father?
When a pun becomes apparent.

What is considered the height of wit?
Tall stories.

witch doctors

When the witch doctor began to sing and dance, what was the missionary's first question?
"What the hex he up to?"

witches

Why do witches ride brooms?
So that they can sweep through the sky.

What do you call a witch who lives on the beach?
A sandwitch.

Why did the witch have trouble writing letters?
She just couldn't spell properly.

What is a witch's favorite plant?
Poison ivy.

How does a witch tell time?
With a witch watch.

What do witches put on their hair?
Scare spray.

wives

What did Father Christmas's wife say during a thunderstorm?
"Come to the window and look at the rain, dear."

Why was the ship's captain disappointed with his new wife?
He took her as a mate, but she turned out to be a skipper.

What did the woodman's wife say to him one day?
"There aren't many chopping days to go before Christmas."

As I was going to St. Ives,
I met a man with seven wives,
Each wife had seven sacks;
Each sack, seven cats;
Each cat, seven kits.
Kits, cats, sacks, and wives,
How many were going to St. Ives?
None—they had just come from there!

wolves

Why are wolves like playing cards?
Because they both come in packs.

If you had to choose between a date with a wolf or a sailor, which is the better?
Watch out for that sailor—he may be a wolf in ship's clothing!

women

What would happen if all the women left the country?
We would have a stagnation.

Why do many men like wanton women?
Because they believe that the heavier a woman is the sexier she is.

Why are some women very much like teakettles?
Because they sing away pleasantly and then all at once boil over.

We've all heard about yes-men, but if you wanted to write a play about a yes-woman what would you call it?
How about "She Stoops to Concur"?

Why do some women in love like the circus?
Because they have an itching for the ring.

In previous generations, why were unmarried women encouraged to stay at home in fine weather?
Because society did not approve of their having a little sun and air until they were married.

Why are young women so partial to sunset and twilight?
Because they are daughters of Eve.

What is the difference between a woman and her watch?
The watch makes a man remember the hours and the woman makes him forget them.

wood

As I was crossing the bridge, I met a man with a load of wood. It was neither straight nor crooked. What kind of wood was it?
A load of sawdust.

woods

Through the woods,
Through the woods I ran,
And as little as I am
I killed a man.
What am I?
An arrow, or bullet.

If you are chased by a bear in a field, how far into the woods should you run to escape?
Halfway—after that you'll be running out of the woods.

words

What word is always pronounced wrong?
Wrong.

What word is there of five letters from which, if you take two away, only one remains?
Stone.

What five-letter word has six left when you take two away?
Sixty.

What is the longest word in the English language?
Smiles. There is a mile between the beginning and the end of it.

What word is there of one syllable which, if you take two letters from it, becomes a word of two syllables?
Plague. Ague.

What word of four syllables represents Sin riding on a little animal?
Synonymous.

I am a word. My first part is a reflection, my second not so much, and my whole none at all.
Thoughtless.

work
What kind of person always hopes for dull work?
A skate sharpener.

Who earns a living without doing a day's work?
A night watchman.

What should you remember if you work in a pickle-packing plant and want to get ahead?
All work and no play makes Jack a dill boy.

Why is someone who works in a gun factory like a pickpocket at a cocktail party?
They both rifle the bores.

world
Why can the world never come to an end?
Because it is round.

What goes all over the world and has but one eye?
A needle.

World's Fair, the
Where is the best place to hold the World's Fair?
In bed.

worms
What did one worm say to the other on meeting in a Dover sole?
"What's a nice worm like you doing in a plaice like this?"

What is worse than finding a worm in an apple?
Finding half a worm.

What does a worm do in a cornfield?
It goes in one ear and out the other.

worry
Why does worry cause falling hair?
When the going gets tough, the tufts get going.

worst
What is the worst thing that can happen to you?
Nothing. If nothing is happening, you're dead!

Or, as the British see it . . .
What is worse than the Devil, better than God, the dead eat it,
and if we ate it we should surely die?
Nothing.

What is the best way to worst an enemy?
Buy him a new suit—then he'll really be worsted!

wrestling

If polo is called the sport of kings, how would you describe wrestling?
The sport of clings.

What is the worst time of year to take up wrestling?
Watch out for the fall!

writers

Why is a good writer of detective stories like an adhesive manufacturer?
He has to operate a clue factory.

Why is he also like one of King Arthur's knights?
He writes wrongs.

Why should every screenwriter be arrested?
He spoils the picture for the rest of the audience.

writing

Why is a sample of handwriting like a dead pig?
Because it is done with the pen.

Is it safe to write on an empty stomach?
Paper works much better.

*Q. A captured **zebra** was fastened to a fifty-foot chain yet he walked a hundred feet. How?*

A. The chain wasn't attached to anything but the zebra.

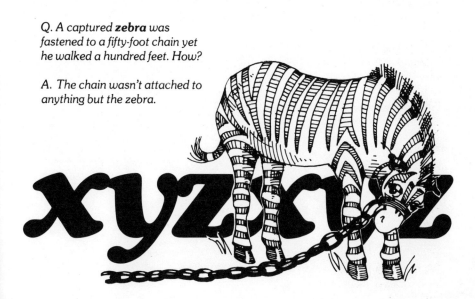

X

When is X the most appealing of letters?
When it is served with bacon.

xylophone

Why is it hard to play the xylophone and stay sober?
You spend all your time running up and down from one bar to another.

Y

Why is a young lady dependent upon the letter Y?
Because without it she would be a young lad.

Why is the letter Y like an unmarried mother?
Because it makes the pa pay.

yachts

Why does a yachtsman have to have strong will power?
Steering calls for stern discipline.

yards

How many feet are there in a yard?
It all depends on how many people are standing in it!

What is bought by the yard but worn by the foot?
A carpet.

Why is 4,840 square yards like a bad tooth?
Because it is an acre.

What is the difference between one yard and two yards?
A fence.

yeast
What will happen if you eat yeast and shoe polish?
You will rise and shine.

yellow
Why did the enemy turn yellow?
They saw that we had our troops all mustard.

What is yellow, soft, and goes round and round?
A long-playing omelet.

yes
What question can always be answered "Yes"?
What does Y-e-s spell?

yesterday
What yesterday was and what tomorrow will be?
Today.

yolks
Which is correct?
The yolk of an egg is white.
The yolk of an egg are white.
Neither. The yolk of an egg is yellow.

yours
What's "yours"?
A scotch and soda, thanks.

youth
What is meant by "the flush of youth"?
Excessive childish use of the toilet.

Z
When is the letter Z not used in Japan?
When Japan is spelled correctly.

zebras
A captured zebra was fastened to a fifty-foot chain yet he walked a hundred feet. How?
The chain wasn't attached to anything but the zebra.

zippers

What was the influence on churches of the invention of the zipper?
They began to get fewer buttons on the collection plates.

zookeepers

Why did the zookeeper run after the lady?
Because she was leaving with a mole on her nose.

Zurich

What is "the gnome of Zurich"?
Zurich doesn't have a gnome. You're thinking of Alaska.

About the Author

John S. Crosbie is president of the Magazine Association of Canada. He is founder of the International Save the Pun Foundation and is the author of *Canada and Its Leaders, Crosbie's Dictionary of Puns, Crosbie's Punned Haiku, The Incredible Mrs. Chadwick,* and *The Mayor of Upper Upsalquitch.* He was named "Punster of the Year" in 1978.